THE MOUNTAIN IN THE SEA

The Mountain in the Sea

POEMS

Victor Hernández Cruz

 COFFEE HOUSE PRESS :: MINNEAPOLIS :: 2006

Coffee House Press books are available to the trade through our primary distrib-utor, Consortium Book Sales & Distribution, 1045 Westgate Drive, Saint Paul, MN 55114. For personal orders, catalogs, or other information, write to: Coffee House Press, 27 North Fourth Street, Suite 400, Minneapolis, MN 55401.

Coffee House Press is a nonprofit literary publishing house. Support from pri-vate foundations, corporate giving programs, government programs, and generous individuals help make the publication of our books possible. We gratefully acknowledge their support in detail in the back of this book.

Good books are brewing at coffeehousepress.org

LIBRARY OF CONGRESS
CATALOGING-IN-PUBLICATION DATA

Cruz, Victor Hernández, 1949–
The mountain in the sea : poems / by Victor Hernandez Cruz.
p. cm.
ISBN-13: 978-1-56689-191-2 (alk. paper)
ISBN-10: 1-56689-191-4 (alk. paper)
1. Title.
PS3553.R8M68 2006
811'.54—DC22
2006012062

FIRST EDITION | FIRST PRINTING
1 3 5 7 9 8 6 4 2
Printed in the United States

Some of the poems in *The Mountain in the Sea*
have previously appeared in the following:

Some of the Haikus were first published in *By Lingual Wholes,* Momo's Press, 1982; *Sniper Logic,* University of Colorado at Boulder; *square one,* Creative Writing Program, University of Colorado at Boulder; *American Diaspora: Poetry of Displacement,* ed. by Virgil Suarez and Ryan G. Van Cleave, University of Iowa Press; The poem "Mongo Santamaria" first appeared in *Bombay Gin,* Naropa lit-erary magazine; *Turnrow,* magazine of the University of Louisiana at Monroe; some of the poems are featured in *Exquisite Corpse,* online magazine ed. by Andre Codrescu.

THE MOUNTAIN IN THE SEA

CONTENTS

Island Waves

To the memory of Barbara Christian (1943–2000)
Caribbean woman from St. Thomas,
she grew up with the waves.
Creative Scholar, Professor,
enduring protagonist of Afro-American
and Caribbean literatures.
Her contributions will endure
the rhythms of her life
always remembered.

Shango—Cabio Sili

"The area qualifies as a natural region, fuzzy about the edges but having common characteristics: it is the rim of land about a mediterranean sea; it is the double corridor between North and South America; and it is the region of tropical climate to the north of the Equator that is stirred by the trade winds."

—CARL ORTWIN SAUER
The Early Spanish Main

"El Caribe es mucho más que el mar que aparece en los mapas. Al mencionarlo, evocamos una constelación de islas, de lenguas y de razas; recordamos colores, aromas, cadencias, ritmos y ritos; anticipamos los tesoros escondidos de una fantasía que desdeña las certezas científicas y las apreciaciones lógicas. Para muchos de los que vivimos sobre sus playas el Caribe es un hecho de la imaginación antes que un área geográfica."

—FERNANDO PICÓ
Historia general de Puerto Rico

O N THE ISLAND YOU FEEL MORE SKY AND WATER. In the age of seashells it was constant Canoa between the Orinoco basin all the way up to the Florida Keys and over to the Yucatán. Things have come out of the sea and have jumped back in. Mostly these poems were written between Puerto Rico and Morocco. Morocco is the land of Amina, my wife, my Mora. These poems were written in English in two places where the English language does not prevail, so writing puts me in a sort of isolation, or exile from immediate circumstances, and becomes a private code. I hope I am translating cultures, as I always feel southern Spain, Andalusia, on the way home to the Caribbean or on the way home to north Africa. These are the places that color my poems; I crisscross them and melt the many fusions that history has knitted through these regions.

I continue here my tribute poems to distinct personalities of art and history, a taste that should highlight my own cultural infusions. They are biographical poems and inspirations based upon the character, whether it is a composer of boleros, or a Muslim philosopher, as is the case with Averroës. For these poems I did a considerable amount of investigation, which I mixed with intuitive elegiac flurries.

If we read the history of the world, we realize that human culture is migration and fusions, that no regions or peoples could be who they are without the contact and assistance from others. Humanity has always been peoples of the sea, waves of migration, languages built on each other: we are more Spanish because of the Arabs, and the Arabs more brilliant because of the Greeks; all of us more scientific because of the Arabs and the Asian Indians. In these two places where I live, the drama of my life is energized among two of the most fused mestizo human societies, the Caribbean and the Maghreb. The most important aspect to me is not the point of political nation (Puerto Rico, the place of my birth, is still a territory with no massive inclination toward self-rule, unique in its adoration of foreign control in the whole world), but the points of cultural confluence. I am a Caribbean mestizo-mulatto and I am aware that my cultural extension is the whole of the Hispanic Caribbean, Santo Domingo, and Cuba, as well as Panama and Venezuela, the Caribbean coast of Colombia, even the Yucatán, and, alas, New Orleans. In terms of geography and shapes, cultural fashions, that is truly immense; I would feel at home in any one of these ports upon the map.

By further extension I feel this sense of Morocco containing many of the same gestures and colors, composures, and musically we are compatible at many levels; the Puerto Rican use of hand drums in the plena reminds me of so many rhythms that I hear in the Plaza Fna of Marrekech with the same style of drums, including improvised sing-song invention on the spot.

The Muslim religion of my Moroccan family and the Christian religion of my Puerto Rican side are both based upon the Jewish prophets; they exhibit the same brilliant abandon to sincere faith in the creator and the same shameful inhibitions. There are of course differences in the manner of prayer and some other spiritual nuances and cultural aspects, like language, but overall we are dealing with a very similar theological orientation.

I melt in both my places through the popular and the traditional weaving questions, practicing upon them the craft of writing, like an artisan forging geometric lines continuously to create a poetry of lyric nerve that is neither popular nor traditional but cultivated and hermetic. It takes an influence from North American poetics which is a definition in which I participate; I am outside the North American mainstream, not to mention mainland, writing in an idiom that should be familiar to North American readers, except that my field is the world below and yonder, set in other languages.

These waves came mostly on the island of Puerto Rico and some that I rode into shore in Morocco. I hope they serve as a bridge over the motion of the water, to help others as the energy, shape, and color has helped me to see differences and distances as exciting, to feel the world as a beautiful mystery. I offer observations and dialogue, guitar melody, and drumbeats to stimulate ideas and questions. These poems have been long planted, taking sun and sometimes hurricane wind: it is my bouquet of flowers from a garden beautiful, sad, happy, and tense. It is the flavors of the things of the world that have come into my grasp. Enjoy the voyage and the aroma.

THE CRUST OF THE ISLAND

Rock is the dance of water,
the sunken pressure of fire,
somewhere deeper water is ablaze,
burning caves subterranean flames,
the barracuda sees a glow. Charges.
Rock-hard music carbonate forming
captured fish bones not fast enough
Wind and fire took them for drum,
Igneris were Adam's feet,
anger and eyesight from Atlantis
forming calcareous motion,
letters from another world frozen in
the minerals.

Could it have been sex sperm whales
charging up my nose the smell of cod
in Spanish
Originating stone plantains just by a lift
in search of fresh air.

Igneri peoples' flesh desires
folded into contours mounds that seed
guayaba red soil dancing the serpentine
opaque green the thrill of magnesium
Giving Chinese to limestone beds of marl
clay stone pillow soft proximity brings
hardness orgasm of shells and corals
spitting out of a calabaza first man
who folded out water the island his back
spine rhythm.
Igneri girl in deepest substrata counting
the sand grain
The rim of the isle is a desert called beach,
we step upon what was once cooked
Red clay of sunken poets
Magi light incense-scrolls text in the compost
of time rotting to be born.

The sun and the moon take turns suckling,
if it all from the water exploded, we are
zilch before time / a zip code district
so deep beyond the pearl eaten by
suck mucous mouth.

And yet the island is a baby
so young geologically just emerged into the
light only 200 million years ago, nada,
in the barbacoa of Allah.
Everything blossomed the tsunami wave
circulated the Atlantic from Iroquois
now Coney Island to the Guanches now
Gran Canarias—Africa baptized
The colossal pool losing stones
for the giants to hop /
Whence earth chichis of Mama
the entire Puerto Rico Trench
nowhere else is this mother deeper
Where the plates scratch move like arms
of something so subtle we dream it
Should the hunchback shaman
shift throw a step wake us into the
future of our past wet tilting Manatí
Holding the sound of the silent volcanoes.

This the trench that has a pull of physical
gravity
the one that swallowed Roberto Clemente
complete with the boxes of clothes and
powdered milk en route to earthquake
victims in Nicaragua

It's a depth that creates a treacherous
silence in the sky above it,
Looking at it from coastal pleasant
allures great palms dance
the invitation toward oblivion,
fathomless attraction,
The curve of Arecibo like Sonia,

her tongue of sedimentary stone
from the mouth core of the Cortillera Central
Her legs stretched toward Cayey
arms once volcanic caress Luquillo,
Geographically what never politics
subdued the North American plate
down below sunken near the gates
of hell,
Where once a cavern contained hot
mineral water,
till a monstrous magma pushed against
its sensitivity,
Ask the priests of Egypt,
or Coabey goddesses that went
To Yucatán Chiapas to dance
upon the perfect Mayan calendar,
for there they knew how to count
the beats of the specks of firmament
fire,
or just ask Sonia's cousin la Cuca
she will tell you how water salt
made her climb palm long.

Merely 45 million years ago
a dot on Kronos' ass,
The orchestra playing took a break,
all that cha cha cha magma
volcanic mambo,
mountaintops of smoke
islands down,
The sculpture was from the northern-
most tip of mofongo pulp,
shape plainly the heart of the
island turf,
the ships with instruments decipher
what is running west
away from the depths of the Caribbean
bowl,
and all such a short time ago
you wonder who walked on

the island first
sidestepping crabs or iguanas,
or if a shrimp brushed a rock
by chance.

Cro-Magnon jaw structure
still in use
chewing fast food gringos bring,
Mayaguez oval finality,
Reefs we come upon cavern deeper
yet.

Now areytos recount through the air
what Bibles and Gilgamesh once spoke,
Noah floating is future still
I sing justified the same,
Belief in water, if there is one
thing I do respect,
if there's one substance I
stand in awe of,
AGUA—EL MAH—WATER
We are its guest and mostly are of,
Mess with thought where it lives
barely language could reach,
Fire is a flight through dark chambers,
Water before and after
Water is what I speculate
Stone sculpture wetness I kiss
don't go in it too deep,
This liquid-earth which came out of
a calabash,
I step upon the shell lightly
not to disturb liquid or bones,
Expect anything while you wait
upon this emerald that emerged
from outside eternal eons
of guayaba pastel crust.

Other Shores

ASILAH
—*to Mohommed Gharbi*

Doors open onto other doors.
Windows floating in the water,
the houses are in the sea,
Rise through some stairs and
the walls are made of fish,
Rushes of saltine breeze,
the coastal rock has darkened
from so much argument with the waves,
From so much beckoning
from the distance that keeps
coming, never to arrive.
You sleep as the waves listen.
The street alone at night
the labyrinth of curves,
spirals of the
seashells,
Makes a sound
medieval doors opening
to mist pressed against
hard walls.

How does the light arrive
into the painting.
The market with its stacks
of fruits
Oranges tangerines like pyramids
upon the carts,
Boxes of dates
sacks of almonds, barrels of spices,
Olives whispering in oil
a vernacular of Arabic/Berber
meanings behind the frames
of customary events spreading
like spiderwebs, till you find
yourself painted into the

corner of a rug.
Boys kick a soccer ball sandals
with bare toes
with head and knees.
Momentarily I fly above the houses
so that I could see from bird's-eye
the curve of the coast,
the garments that hang upon
roof lines
Rugs hanging from balconies
taking the fresh of the wind
Pillows also as if to clean them
of all dreams.
Air given to all things to blow
away all malice that might have
imbued upon.

Mufti tales through the streets
the personal history of corners,
The moon of the community,
All the new structures that are old.
We walk between tiles and water
esplanade occasional splashes of
el mah.
Mufti's house is Moroccan traditional
sofas and pillows
Run along the entire room
hugging the light blue sky walls.
Figurines behind glass cabinets,
Round silver platters almost
like mirrors of geometry.
The tiles with shapes found
in a prism through which a
dark pink light has danced.
The patterns say the same thing,
repeat themselves like time.
Just like in the world
where there are so many Fatimas,

And the sky is full of so many night
Laylas who claim that all their
brothers are Sa'ids.

Opening doors to rooms we
didn't know were there,
Which were not available
before this time,
Suddenly our hands are full
mint and almonds, sesame,
A mist of rose water
In the room where the furniture
is air
floating above alfombra designs.
I know now I am with my people
The song rising from earthen
Asilah
Reminding us that the key is
within us
It is within our pants in the pocket
almost in the hand:
The verse says it:
"The moon will be red in a dark
blue O sky visible from a room
of silver letters"
For that reason the night sings
for the travelers to play their new
strings in the imagination's palace
where they are flickering sparks
A flower made a thousand times
over
In the squares of infinite tiles,
in the sand that goes toward
the water,
Which cleans before opening
the words.

In the dark silence of the aurora,
those who sleep deep in dream

Must be by now metaphors
waving toward the fountain
pen of future poets.
From Asilah I take with me
the memory of the hidden rooms
Sudden doors,
gifts of a singular glimpse
the sea of forever morning.

FEZ

In the madrasah the colors of
the book of verses are studied,
the rhythm and the sound,
How to enter into a book,
the room of many doors,
the fountain of water
The lips repeat it.
There are rooms within which
there is nothing but tiles
and rugs of blue flowers,
To focus all movement
away from objects
It all leads to oblivion,
it is not the eyes but
the vista
That page after page,
the students do not see
their hands
The letters become musk
Float.

The candles lit in the
room of the body,
The museum of flesh,
The flavor of memory.

We walked through Fez
as if a form of music
Andaluz classic,
vertical violins marching
a crescendo of tambo rhythm,
Perpendicular reptiles
through the circuit of the streets.
Coming upon the alleys
of the tailors,
All of them men with their

delicate hands,
Tempos of great patience,
a kindness within the
Cool task of artisan fingers
A thread of voluntary love
stitch by stitch through
the mint tea.
Caftans hang like flags,
the designs near the wrist
ovals with no beginnings
or ends,
endless becoming, circles,
exhibit their awesome detail.
For women there was silk
as the vendor said:
So that even when they are dressed
they are naked.
Flesh is not seen
it is only touched.
Garments flying off the walls
in every corner a hanger
a hook with some textile,
How is it that they compose
algebra through so much thread.
We are looking at things inside
from the seed, the plant
the flower out,
Perceive through the water
the lines of the leaf,
Everything is water through the
street,
Which is outside yet
a corridor enclosed,
Narrow passageways
Through which we transfer
along with donkeys of freight.
On the larger avenues
Camels stare as if recognizing.

We come to the street
where they sell nougat,
Nuts have acquired sweetness,
in a sculpture of gummy paste,
or hard stone,
Almond and cashew unite
lose some of their identity
to enhance the tongue.
They have them in blocks,
chop them with hatchets,
some shine like edible
glass.
We buy a bag to continue
on the carousel.

It is getting late when we come
to the area of leather,
Its smells of belly hide
its texture of deep mahogany,
tinges of cinnamon papaya,
purses, bags sway in the evening
breeze
Along with the cántico
of the seller.

We make circles and descend
to what seem like caves,
passing curves and homes
windows from which pop
faces intoned and composed;
A mouth of Bedouin lips,
Syria mixed with the
cheeks of native Berbers,
Flesh lighter through this
Fez of artisans,
platters of silver ingrained
with octagons triangles
squares entanglements
Like the streets that we

now ascend toward a new
sky of virgin darkness
violated by points of fire.

The night light makes
the homes sing with a
white that yellows.
The mosques stand up
like bottles of perfume
upon the line of the sky,
the depth of the shadows
lean everywhere from
view of higher turf,
the infinite eternal panorama.
Sound is invisible
we do not see the musicians
that rise from low contentment.
Amina's hands come out of the
melody,
The Fez of darkness totals,
you can see something,
what streetlights and crescent
moon offer,
The rest you have to imagine.

AL–MAGHRIB

I lived in the old medina of Rabat, Morocco, known as Sweka, for eight months staying in a couple of hotels, first in the Hotel Dormir, run by a French woman who had converted to Islam. The bed in the room took up all the space; I had just space enough to walk to a sink and a closet. The next place I stayed was the Hotel Kasbah deeper into the medina and funkier, wooden door windows swung open onto a courtyard patio decorated with blue azulejos. While there I wrote poems into a journal. These are some of the fragments.

THE MEDINA POEMS

I.
Listening to the sounds of Arabic
melting in my afternoon ears
walking through the medina's nougat taste,
Amina's hands are my hands
Slowly the awareness of significance
comes, syllables that bring hints,
a flavor in the word, henna kissing
hands waving the new sounds,
a smooth turning opens like petals
in the air of so many people
between me and my ears, the
oven is making adverbs for my
movements, the flowers are taking
light, "Lah arabia" I tell someone
"Esnew?" Amazed the
next words are smiles or the palm pressed against the heart.
The night sounds like "Fil-lill"
Lilac—and as Layla fulfills the darkness,
a sound in the air. Concentration
of the ears a silent growing
words that link into phrases,

Against the walls of the Sale Medina
older than el Morro of Old San Juan,
I have in both of these aged walls
listened for runaway slave words,
for contraband nouns pronounced
when the priest and the qadi are asleep.
It's almost like a word is a place
that you can enter and dwell,
Repeating it till erased in a dream,
the body no longer,
I enter a house of women dressed
in amber skin shining like bottles
crepuscular dim light touching them my hands
become flames jellabas become tamarind
husk color Entering the Orinoco of curves and
flesh the same gourd hands play la'ud.
I divide into the original clay of Adam,
The music is in the calligraphy
With the red moon floating in the
sky raying into the adobe walls, the scarves
and black blankets colors
Orange/blue Miró might have through
sheer chance stepped on one of
the letters, which look like men and
women in Eros, or the desert sand
dunes forming unbecoming creating this
way the people who live within the wind,
the animals and the flowers
The trees not seen are concealed in echoes,
Fragrance that links the verses,
The alif of primordial creation,
the prayers salat— "Allah akbar"
Folding, bending, falling
into a river like a bushel of bamboo leaning,
the quill of clear ink encounter with the Merciful
like a stream
Flowing back to you before a door
Opens.

Look in the neighborhood Hassan
through a window I behold
the cross of the Catholic cathedral,
Six birds fly in frenzy above
the dome,
The sky has thrown on a gray slip
to hide its "kind of blue skin"
Miles Davis across Morocco from
the flower market with a subterranean
echelon where they sell almonds and
dates.
Blue and orange jellabas flow with
John Coltrane sax.

Our arte in heaven king be thy
come,
On jet ski river making holes
in the water,
Italian cars parked in Rabat
along the Burrengreg River
watching night show spectacle
the young emperor still without
Queen gliding through liquid.

What are the girls I went to
high school with in Spanish Harlem
doing walking around Morocco?
I swear I saw Sonia Ramirez, Frances,
Carmen, Sandra in the medina

How that happen?
Did they come here to get old?
Minerva with the taste of Bazooka
gum tongue still beautiful as she stares
from under a veil
The last time of her steps
the bolero blouse the Fu Manchu
Woolworth's perfume,
Rising up a stoop on 109th St.

Last night I heard songs in Hay Salam
coming from windows
They were songs to the angels
who carry the crystals of poetry
across the realms transparent toward
manifestation.
The night is cool
the gift of the rooftops
concrete words skid
Make me aware of darkness
drift of perfume streets camouflage desire,
Against the white caftan
the black shapes of the ink. Look.

Another sign that we share blood
when the boleros came on
It reminded everyone of everything
The hope of love across continents
conquered and destroyed / the sword
plucks the guitar, Omara Portuondo
bellows what begging flowers in the eyes.
Further north fado conceals
us through Portugal the voice shaking
for the lover.

All these are my lands
wherever the sand cries
echo of deep-sea tears.
The new words are ancient,
in your hands
moist new meaning.

2.

Does the Arabic sound like jazz scat
Betty Carter flowing out of a caftan
exploding at the tips of words,
In circles adding to say the
same, necklace scat of five-language squash
rising with the mint tea
in the hands of the Berbers in the courtyard.
Out of the sea prehistoric columns
visible again, whole walls inscribed
rise with bone alphabet time.
Pictures of past music
the bones still dancing.
The Bronx comes melodious to Rabat,
like one time Jerry Gonzalez said
that Dizzy Gillespie asked him where
the three–two clave went
It's still there he told him
At the bottom
Patato cook at the bottom
let the top stay raw.
In the music it feels like you are
spinning, you are moment to
moment, If you stop to listen
to another instrument the horse can
throw you off, if you jump a beat,
entangle the clave, the whole dance
floor could shift / A red sun falling
into the ocean / another moment
the moon is broadcasting through Marrakech
card reader
someone nearby eats fire /
In Loiza Aldea a Taino fritter spills
onto the Bomba.
I was looking for a watch
with Arabic numerals all over the
medina
Suddenly I recognize another Arabic
expression in a neighboring conversation

Nothing with me just two
girls chatting, one says the word
wejet and I flash on the number, the one
the two nymphs were talking about.
The bus crosses the Burrengreg River
I am going to Hay Salaam
Pass the favelas where there is
no electricity or running water,
the people have genius to
put electricity in some of the
huts the TV screen can be seen from
the bus. The teenaged girls are the
ones who fetch water in the public
fountain across the street dressed
as if Botero had painted their jellabas
dresses and head scarves
in vibrant hues.

3.
Night is falling a mixture of smoke and
dust
slants into faint shadows
a blue that purples,
Carts driven by donkeys criss-
cross behind the main street,
whipped by little boys
One hand the whip
with the other they eat
tangerines
They continue up into further
Hay Salam
Where the pavement ends,
The dirt begins
Wooden planks leading into
main entrance, street vendors,
children meshing fleeting barefoot or sandals
throughout the street dense with action
We visit rug makers
in cavernous quarters

They serve us mint tea in glasses
with golden geometric rim
designs, the children of the
household all knew a few words
in Spanish,
A courtesy and a happiness
to see us as guests in their house
Against a wall was a huge
rug-making machine taking up
most of the little living room.
It was Friday of couscous aroma windows
later we walked back home through
fragrances of roasting almonds and horse
manure
A cool breeze through darker dark
night streets
without lights strolling ducking
horse-driven carriages full of women
hijab eye laughter,
now and then an open window
showed us blue and orange
interiors
and the shadows of those who
squatted upon rugs.

4.
A well-danced calligraphy jumped
from a medina wall and took
me by the hand,
Was it past the restaurant
where couscous costs twenty dirhams
Never bread with couscous,
always water the waiter brings,
or past the bakery with the
oven sunk into the ground,
fed wood from behind
lumber-stacked alley
Adjacent the mosque whose floor
is straw mats,

adding to the construction of
silence
within the still
air of the prayer. Stillness
Whenever it was that the alif
became part of my shoulder
it made a sound down into my hands,
As walking down the stairs that spill
out the bay,
Heard the wood of history in the
word *boat,*
that separated water between
Algeciras and Sale,
When the Guzmans, Ben Yusefs,
Ben Barka, Perez family trees
surfed back away from the
Swords that were made in Toledo.
Back in the hotel I read Ibn Arabi
Wisdom of the Prophets
and picture him in Seville eating
sweet almond nougat
Dreaming of books left behind
on Murcia shelves.

5.
Sounds are trapped in words
walking through the narrow streets,
the colors of the language
Walking by so many tongues,
Arabic, French, Spanish, German tourist.
My hotel room is painted pink
reminding me of family apartments
of campesino psychedelics.
Afternoon sky and sardines
Mediterranean breeze
Reading poets from the Caribbean
the cadence of poem dances.
Over the murmur of
the medina merengue from Santo Domingo

I jump from hotel bed
running out to the street
Thinking a carnival had come
through the Atlantean substratum
a good ripiaó, one those merengues
upon-beach-out
It was contraband cassette from
one of the many music store
holes-in-the-wall.

The streetwalkers are pressed
sardines in cans
In the patterns the shuffle of the
feet
Words pierce the silence
Slower down to a vibration
to its moisture
The sex of the flower
The petal virgin
The bronze incarnation
Back in hotel with round
roll of bread and water
All I have is water and flower
I listen again to Pedro Mir, Santo Domingo poet
"Viaje a la Muchedumbre"

*"There is a country in the world
located upon the very line of
the sun,
Which has its origin in the night"*

Through the window comes
chatter into my sleep,
deeper waves dream province
Tall royal palms, a dinosaur
that eats coconuts
Mulatas so gold
like a mixture of Mandingo with
Taino cheeks a bridge to Bangladesh,

A flowered red skirt barefoot
A club in San Pedro de Marcoris,
The jukebox spills *café en el campo,*
Juan Luis Guerra wants it to rain
coffee, CAWAH from the heavens,
Ethiopian beans,
A voice calls the new day
out of the shadowy rumbas
What was it all
just a little pasture of time back,
Dreaming?

6.

The bottom of the Atlantic:
Ridges, caves, floating apes,
Blue rocks, orange grass,
The antiquity of the poetry
on the bed of the mermaids
Sea horse in the coconut
plena at the end of the palms
The "Blue La'ud" played by the
green fingers of Friday
a cloth that covers the sky
as the harmonics
walk objects out of nowhere,
All day hungry and thirsty,
Walking my foot in the olas wave,
Olé,
Back through the medina of
Ramadan—no one is eating
Only swallowing saliva—
Everything is focused
On creation producing creatures
In most seas we don't observe,
Creation is demanding
shapes to walk out of perfume.
Passing the chants coming from
the dome
The poetry inside testicular generation,

My window is full of syrup,
Honey is pouring in,
Queen Mama is cleaning the
clouds
I am reading a note on al-Jabir
the chemist of Baghdad
He said:
you have to walk everything through,
experiment, actually mix the liquids
and the fumes
otherwise there is no chemistry
And the air does not open.

7.
One day in a winter
that was colder than anyone ever
felt
This is not true this cold is freak
I jumped and had to buy a coat
on the street of contraband
In a men's store I picked up
a scarf
Shooo I was freezing in Africa
The weather was a Visigoth-Iberian
invasion—a wind from the north
with a good push.
Having gone to Hay Salam to
eat with Amina
She made eggplant spicy and
a tangine of fish that looked
like a Luis Hernández Cruz
abstract painting on a silver platter.
Mint tea for the chill.
Coming back that night
Walking along the old
wall of the medina
It starts to rain—I hear
distant thunder—it pours
Like big buckets being spilled,

A wind comes out of nowhere
wants to take my umbrella out of my hands,
It breaks the nylon—I am holding
the skeleton,
I rush toward a door to survive,
Spirals of wind keep coming
I am wet as if I had
just dived into the ocean.
Got back to the hotel,
the managers said they
couldn't recognize me,
I came covering my head with my
black coat—they thought I was
a horse loose in the night
or a beast that materialized,
The next day I just stared out
the window at the azulejos
A sky so blue
gave light to the
poetry book of San Juan
de la Cruz. Water and dancing
wind.

8.
In a profound deep cave
I was in North Africa dreaming
with the Lower East Side of
Manhattan
Dreams don't obey geography
Maybe some face I walked by
without noticing later I recalled
the mestizo air the way they
mix Berber–Mali blood the
way Puerto Rico mixes Bantu and
Spanish all to become the same
features of a history.
I dream with my street friend Chino,
who is not from China but
from Bayamón and lived on Ninth Street
near the Avenue D projects.

He had the loveliest cousins
we went to visit around Pitt Street
around the park with a pool
Around a library and a school—
Their parents were not home,
we had some rum with tamarind
juice sold clandestinely in a Sixth Street
bodega
We challenged the girls to drink,
and they said like nothing
Around three o' clock
and their mom pop in Jersey City
across the Hudson—
They had these little shot cups
that had figures of sultanas
engraved in red.
We started going around once
each
Music from another apartment
and the fragrance of incense
used to clean house of bad
spirits
And then a bolero then
we danced, the door open
seeing through to a wall where hang
black turbaned heads they call *Congos*
two black faces with gold earrings
it was the last floor next door to the roof
Going there we see iguanas
and out on the Manhattan skyline
rows and rows of palms sprouting
from roofs
all around deep pink sky.
Images traveling are a gift,
music or perfume awakes them
upon my body sunken in the painted
limestone of Moroccan
sleep caverns.

Portraits

RAFAEL HERNÁNDEZ

Born through exact rhythms in Aguadilla
north coast Puerto Rico
A beam of light through the balcony
of the modest wooden house.
With the cooperation of the wind,
through a side street
lifts the skirts of sirens
who have walked out of the sea,
Onto the plaza so near,
wearing Atlantean seashells
for earrings,
Rafael saw them magnified
everything twice.
The charcoal circles of their eyes
Becoming the light of his songs.

Island beauty inside the resonance
of the guitar
With words he saw the way the
mountains see themselves.
Creator's eyes.

It was not by chance
the place of birth
He pinpointed the tropical night
composer of sound,
the birds like bells of glass,
The people in the lyrics
the hands and the landscape,
An ox walks through the rim
of the eyelid,
Cinema through the lips.

When he left for other lands
he took the trees with him,
put rivers in his pockets,

Condensed amapolas into his pores,
a suitcase full of fruit.
He'd be sitting in Harlem
listening to caribe birds,
Congolese rhythms
came to his guarachas,
Conchitas of his youth
danced for him in Mexico.
They scaled the pyramid walls
dancing plenas and bombas
for Quetzalcoatl.
On 116th Street he saw a
guaraguao fly over a cane field.

From the bottom up the people
art themselves spilling finally
Back down to the root of
the popular romance.

Rafael wore his hats like poetic meters,
coplas decimas
The declaimers art with strings.
He traveled ragtime jazz
with Jim Europe's band
Soldiers in Paris.
Improvising swing through danza
cadence.

What sings in the Americas
passes through his filters.
His home was all the countries
of the tropical bolero,
Pan-mestizaje like Bolívar's invitation.

Like Dante and Cervantes
his lyrics reached toward an
impossible love,
An odyssey, a yearning to touch
her, dreaming awake.

This illusive girl was also
his nation,
Each lyric points to the map,
her impossible yet necessary creation.
The countryside coming
to the cities made his songs,
gestures in the gardens where
Flowers dance with drought
Dry in the mirror of history,
In the epoch of his rhymes.
It is the movement of Rafael
with his load of viands
Toward civilization
Full of a place without legitimacy,
false authority,
beautiful without insignias,
A green mineral floating upon blue
waters,
A pebble of mother earth,
A womb
A nation becoming in his words,
giving birth
To the children of eternal liberation.

FELIPE RODRIGUEZ
—to *Juan Belen Concepción abogado de Aguas Buenas*

Desire flames treason
in the morning of the river
flowing with roses.
Their eyes in his voice
their thorns in his hands.
A taino cemis strolls out of
a bar singing,
The timbre rough and drunk
spiced with the liquor of thoughts,
Sharp and raspy
a nervous kind of waving.
Adventurous golondrina bird
of sad wings,
Their choreography prior to the rain,
a monsoon of remembered love
entanglements,
A lament through evenings dressed
in gowns,
Purple sequins syllables of ruffles,
high-heel shoes dangling from fingers
dragging toward beds of secrets.
Seagram's Seven and cigarette smoke.
Felipe and the Trio Los Antares
making radio waves,
High-rises for broken hearts
vein slashers in cathedrals.
Thin mustache wavy black hair
Arawak cheek perched.
We dance boleros in the stark
azulie of the ocean,
Throughout the fifties of motion,
the age of banishment.

They say the guitars first came
aboard a ship called the *Marine Tiger,*

Into the Brooklyn docks of immigrants' lust,
passage of humid vapors through urban
hallways,
Unbecoming the cement between the bricks,
the screws of the wrought iron of the stairs.
Inside windows walls of strawberry,
kitsch angels bordello furniture,
Cabaret lamps dimly visible.
In a room we see the empty bed,
The East River enters through an
open window.
In the veins floats the river Yaguez.
The radio a large Emerson of marble
plastic,
Felipe's voice floating like cigar smoke,
lamenting through all necessity.
He chiseled in our childhoods
the memoirs of a nation,
The memory of first love.
agricultural zones of tropical
geography.
The years pass they must
But Felipe "La Voz" singing "China Hereje"
never goes out of style.
I've heard it in the future of Hilo, Hawaii
near an active volcano.
Love is a dance of generations,
the same illusion just waiting
for the bodies to arrive.
It takes a glimpse to create a galaxy,
the future in our sight,
It is the same eyes praised in Andalusian
Trovas,
Gazelles that aim and fire
throughout all epochs of desire.

Now in the tavern of bohemian friends,
we sing the songs against our wills,
Betrayal the same way we saw it once,

as if the past is in the future,
The same spears have pierced
other people under the drama of
similar moonlit nights.

The singers sip the ruby wine,
serve more cane the poet springs,
Recalling the kisses of the mountains
trembling with pleasure.

They say that the lament
belongs to the entire desert.
Sometimes when you least expect it
the song of your memories
comes from a distant house,
It burns a blue light inside of you,
hands caress the invisible hair.
Walking toward the balcony
through a window
a curtain is pushed aside
exposing an ancient face.

Ah, it is a tree that sings.

SYLVIA REXACH I
—*para Ate Maria Monserrate*

Along with what you respire
Is a voice
salty and right out of the sea.
The horizon what the whole eye
can eat,
Clouds we confuse with mountains,
distant buildings Santurce, Rio Piedras
antennas upon everything her songs
pour like rich tamarind pulp.
The entire oval of the island imbibes,
the coquettish flames
The florid arboreal gives birth to
so much possibility of encounter,
insisting like the waves of the sea,
The sand we lay upon is sound,
something so soil
so purple
so moisture.
Mountains suffer their separation
in the panorama of sex,
Roble trees shine as if in orgasm,
the roots of the plants receive the
seeds of other planets
they occasion to grow with us,
listen to the vegetation that travels
with the guitar,
A call-and-response to the hurt,
gold tooth gypsy's drink café
at la Bobonera.
A chorus repeats the humidity
two spoons of sugar pour into
the black liquid of night
to dance with the saucer's
bitter occupation.

Seashells feel the lyrical pain,
the woman composing a butterfly
She wrote on gardenia petals
with the sharp pencil of her soul.
Oblivion returns to memory
Through those journeys where
the captain of the boat sailed,
a ship lost in blue desire.
Her metaphors of liquid
tongue upon the flesh,
the bolero is in Jupiter,
From the bay of San Juan
we see it's sixteen moons
Full.
We are the text of lament
she inquired so much of,
the wound opened and luminous.

From an open window
a woman sits
She is made of jasmine and salt,
A flower of fire instinct of the birds,
she jots down words that
have eyes
They stare back up at who
writes them into melody.
Her hands are rosy
spilling a lilac ink,
Clouds of tenderness
outside the window,
It rains one more time
upon our memories.

SYLVIA REXACH II
—a la memoria de Angela María Dávila

And there when you breathe it
a voice with her words
Covers everything with a film
a cloud
As if the whole country
the whole island oval
Floats on the sea of incantation
with a flirting of love's possibilities,
A rising of the ocean waves,
the sand we lie upon is sound
our primordial nakedness,
A forest
so purple
so burgundy
A screaming lamenting greenness
of so much rum in ice.
All mountains hurt a separation,
boulders and bushels in the panoramas
of all sex,
Roble trees as if in orgasm
with a lighter tinge of shade.
Radiating this fecund interior
into distant planets,
Galaxies seem to be among us
full of a sad sweetness.
A compassion for the moon and
the tears of its inhabitants
Just rises with the vegetation
of her limericks.
Traveling with Caribbean air.

We see that even seashells hurt
spilling the salt of their caverns,
Gardenia petals carry the weight
of sharply piercing pencils,

They recall our memory
Disposed at the gates of treason,
out in high sea
Where a captain's ship
Sails with the wind of our love.
A horizon we caress
Figurines dissolve with our touch.
Her songs are broadcasting in Jupiter
with its sixteen full moons.
A rain shower
coming from the blue sun sky
Celebrating, they say, the wedding of
witches.

In her songs silence sings,
listening
We hear the scratching of someone
writing
by the light of available pain.
She inquired so much of the wound,
heed the open ache
the salt of such luminosity.

From a corner table
a woman of salt and jasmine,
Of instinct feline,
sits writing
Words that stare back at who
produces them,
At who creates them for melody,
hands that are the stems of roses
writing the subtle itches felt by skin flower
Leaning into the tenderness
of the sky,
Which downpours, once again
into our memories.

TRIO LOS CONDES

Lyre and voice
the ancient serenade
Strings right below myth.
A circle of naked flesh
from the pores comes
the a capella of the Greek
chorus, the Taino Areyto flute
in the dance.
The Polynesian hands of
word waves.
Fingers tracing songs
in the wind.
The harmony creates columns
Each one a color a position
Celestial,
Bodies and objects that have
become sound.
I see plates and saucers
enclosed behind glass,
Small shot glass,
a magnificent oval bottle
of brandy,
Men walking through bluish
plastic curtains
Wearing thin ties and silky
suits.
All blue motion, red dance
the chains of Andalusia
broken loose,
What caramel would sing
if given a mouth.
In Cuba the rumba slowed down,
oil of the drummers' hands,
following the lament of the voice,
a mass tribute to the female form
The moon coming down as nickels

for the nickelodeon
Push H-7
Los Condes sing. "Amor de mis amores"
and bring back a skinny Agustín Lara
sitting in the margins of Rubén Darío's
poems
From San Francisco to New York,
a guitar sticks out of a '57 Packard
Moving through streets that are hills
open highway Interstate 10
all the way heartbreaking voyage
To the smog of the east coast
pipes.

They were the counts of a
monarchy of boleros,
For inspiration Pedro Flores flowers
the same,
The bridge of a woman's eyes
The sense of her yellow dress.
Not philosophy of ideas but
the Eros of touch
Skin lyrics
Boleros are flesh poetry
They respire the air you are,
in the distance of oblivion,
recall the picture of all the sweet
truth that floats in the lake of
her eyes,
That this caress was the night star
of your walk coming to my adobe
Toward my heart orphaned of kisses,
amor does not part through eternities,
Have we guessed the clear beauty
of who shines
Who trembles in a voice
The words that belong to men
ink upon the papyrus-woman,

Rhapsody that converts black
hair into white roses.

We've got to have the world
the soil and its birds.
Walk through paths
of folding bamboos
Bring songs
through deserted streets.
We want the ports of the Americas
visible and flagrant
bongos in the undercurrent
moving like ships
below the wings of the strings.
The kiss from the window
reaching the street eye.
Pageantry-Ceremony
People who allow themselves
to be penetrated by words,
Suggestion of freshly brewed desire
sacrificing bodies to the songs
Convinced of illusion.
Such is what Los Condes bring
a memorial pastry of harmonious illusions
songs climbing walls of bricks
Entering through the open window
Into a head that momentarily lifts
from a pillow
only to settle back into the abyss.

MIRÓ

a Néstor Barreto
designer of poems
cohort in aesthetic contraband
through the outlaw mountains

He looked through the prisms
made of the crystal eyes of children,
Honduran children playing with
the fabrics of their Mayan hands
through the almond tree-covered coast.
Vera Cruz tattlers beholding
piñatas for the first time,
East Harlem kids alive with sound
living on 100th street 1957,
Colors of the apartments
French pastry.

He was a dinosaur inside of
a cave making sculpture with the
Swings of his tail
In the dark not to be seen till
fire was invented.
From which he went and set
mud ablaze,
Clay flowing through his hands
a fat woman belly with an orifice
For the twilight star.
The secret alphabet of random
tree branches,
Gazing through the Japanese
calligraphy the haiku brush of insects.
Magnified bees, flamingos, macaws,
suddenly upon the horizon frame
of the sky.
A flower would rise out of terror,
Flames in the bottom of the art.

His Neolithic strokes in the water
air that wants to become rock.
All Catalonia under the darkness of
Monseratte—La Virgin Morena
that April 20th, 1893, baptized his
pupils, took them to
The Caribbean off of Haiti
the salt of tropical water and
the fish of multicolores.
Observing his paintings is like
snorkeling out of water.

The algebra of Islam,
the ruins of language,
Symbols found on insect wings,
Molecule paso doble glass bottom
of microscopes,
The inside of flowers,
the concept of birth in flight,
the blueprints for feathers,
A caterpillar's aesthetics of design,
The dreams of snakes.
Boxes of cartoons jumping
through fresh vegetables.
Dancing fruit;
stellar words visual through
the telescopes of his childhood.
A chance for chance to see
itself
In the scribble lavender of amoebas
now larger than our bodies.
The wardrobe of a clown,
Indian saris dancing through desire.
Persian rugs airplanes connecting flights
to watermelon breasts.
Above Barcelona clouds of
Guatemalan skirts,
A subterranean society jumps to
the surface

Reptilian legs, the foot of a toad
walking malanga and calabaza vine
roots, guayaba ink
Across the snow of the Arctic.

His peasant face
like a white moon
The hand mischievous of all
thought dancing toward
Worlds of uncreated forms
dancing with an eye
located in his palm.

EISENHOWER

How did the bold skull of Eisenhower enter my life,
his head like the moon inside the black-and-white
television sets of the tenements.

Caribbean mountain Spanish phonetics
came up with versions of his name,
who could pronounce such letters?
To some it sounded like "ice in shower" others
said "eye in hour" listening
to the English as if it were music you see,
in the morning of immigration.
Simultaneously Trio Los Panchos lifted
curtains at the Teatro Puerto Rico in the Bronx.

His D-Day European theater performances
still lingering below and above the Popeye
cartoons.
Animation of bombs coming out of the
East River, newsreels of a recent past
Europe's barbarous cold murder
at the same time my grandmother's
brown hands spliced tobacco leafs
in the tropics.

In the apartments of the immigrants
Straw hat brown skeletons stood
next to wooden houses
Flamboyans in black and white
drooping onto the zinc roofs framed in photos
upon shelves staring out the windows
at the snow.
I fancied missiles shooting out of
Hopalong Cassidy's black sombrero,
Coco spilling out of an ink jar
onto the green lush forest of my memory.

We materialized like wild calabaza
foliage into the urban sprawl.

Eisenhower was one of the first faces
we came upon beaming out of the
television.
The king of a new land
That did not feel like earth,
but like boxes of cement
Reaching into a dim gray sky,
We found so many people
already screwed and nailed
into the walls
Immigrants from holocaust
barbed wire
terror still in their eyes
and in the nervous lilt
of their fragmented inglish.

At first we saw the place without words
it was just image and sound,
not knowing the names of things
in their local whats,
We ate the scenery with our eyes
without pronouncing it.
Practicing the sensation of newly
occupied syllables.

What was Eisenhower saying
coming out of the radio,
A line of tanks lined up as words,
splattering into our Caribbean ears
of amphibian melodies.
So many birds left their nest
falling into severe industrial
gravity.
Fruits showed up behind cellophane.

Along with the Korean War,
thick cans of Rheingold beer,
A chocolate syrup in a jar called Bosco,
Willie Mays in the outfield,
Juicy Fruit girls from the suburbs,
serial novelas through Spanish radio,
In the public schools we did
bomb drills,
Diving under the tables in tune
to the sirens from local fire stations.

It was the cinema of arrival
Eisenhower was the star of the movie.
As my English got better
the old bold man disappeared
we saw him no longer.
Parrots kept arriving from the tropics,
piece by piece colored feathers
into the northern drizzle.
Lizards came through bamboo shoots,
Seeds from the center of guavas
tamarind of abandoned soil.
The city skyline became melted
vocabulary
Reaching into the sky's efforts
to become blue.

VIGO MARTIN

In a city that now floats
in a bottle,
In a dimension outside
of the census,
within walls that were unregistered,
there was a painter,
Who performed his roll
like the Taino cave etchers,
the pyramid illustrators of
Mexico,
the scribblers of hieroglyphs.
Vigo painted the hallways
of the tenements,
While through the air
he flew upon a white horse,
Or smoked hashish for
his desert camel through
Moroccan tubes.
He painted rocks
which were heavy art.
Loose bricks were found
by landlords containing
Antillean pictographs.
An artisan of the streets,
whose smooth knowledge of
many angles
Made more lines visible
through the old face
of the barrio.

Against colorful bodega windows,
bright candy stores,
the epoch of the pachanga

Deep in the clubs of night
under the world

In the submetropolis of need,
against walls merely holding up.
Once we spoke of the art
of survival,
of loose lions and hungry tigers,
He painted lizard instincts
along imaginary river bamboo,
Frozen eye sockets
containing tar and northern ice.
We recognized how we were
packed in the chance of numbers,
ciphers in the wintry spread,
noses popping out of sardine cans,
We spoke against the doo-wop of
The Paragons Meet the Jesters
Till dawn brought
a blue light upon
roofs—the city skyline bricks steel
edges jagged in the wind.
In a conference of the stoops
he maintained that *Dulces Labios*
Mayaguez was his origin,
he spoke of sweet mangoes,
plena pulp,
Touching trees in honor
of the Tainos of his hands
stationed deep in his bark,
with his left hand where a tattooed
cherry blossomed.

Vigo made a collaboration
between survival and creativity,
He stored objects that came with
the wind,
Had a cellar full of broken gadgets
portions that could insert into
any malfunction,
A bazaar in search of a dictionary
of shapes and proportion.

He brushed himself like
freezer ice Halka brilliantine shine,
never alone always with a
prehistoric beast.
As evidence that I was there
on this other planet
I still maintain a rock
which he painted against
the laws of gravity
Now a paperweight
grounding the poetry of the tropics
Against the flight of the east trade
winds.

THE HARPTONES
—*for David Henderson*

I want a Sunday kind of love
When yet a child I felt the walkers of the city.
I felt it in the content of the wind,
whatever makes bricks harmonize,
The clatter of street feet.
Sweaters the color of raspberries
disappearing down basement chambers
it looked like gumbo,
The gathering of esqueletos
leather coats and hats in the dark,
fine slow movement set in red light.
Not far the Williamsburg Bridge
Suspense toward deeper Brooklyn,
where at the Fox Theater
Slick guys with Cordovan shoes
in the new guise of conservatives
Listen to Murray the K call out
Little Anthony and the Imperials.
The Bopping Balarinos danced with
their debs in the shadows of the balcony.

A capella was affordable mouth
the studio the echo of the hallways,
Tenements or housing project,
dreamers would be chanting:
All night long
All night long
All night long
to finger snaps.

This was the invisible inner city
shadows in doo-wop
Did you ever have a "Coney Island Baby"
Pier 13
The Himalayan ride

under the boardwalk
Sway like the waves to the
Harptones "The Shrine of Saint Cecilia"
Tonalities of Black/Boricua ears
framed in a velvet melt.
It brings back pictures of streets
whistles, schoolyards, Impalas,
The first fingers in the bush.
Shoe shine and satin
jackets folded and held in the
arm on a horizontal slant
While the eyes scoped the
distant avenue sizzle.
What put Pucho & the
Latin Soul Brothers to cook.

The Harptones took more space
had more bass,
Slow honey amber spilling
from the roofs.
Shoes shuffled on brilliant
circular designs of the linoleum,
Quiet nervous skirts exhibiting
knees
The new sensation of girls bare
summer backs
Exploding through sweaty fingers.
The crackling of air pockets
of the Chiclets tumbling within mouths
aspiring tongue kisses.

Were they singing underwater,
or was a horse doing bass,
A depth so essential like scratching
the bones in grind.

Where has all that sound
and the figures it produced
gone to?

Where did the sharp onslaught
of reality take them.
I see screens in dreams
that bring back the harmony,
The moments of passage,
rituals of initiation.
And it is always:
A Sunday Kind of Love . . .

NORO MORALES

Trumpets and saxophones
flapping like wings of roof
pigeons circulating above
the buildings, below
the beautiful summer
clouds the Mohicans
Gave pipes full of eyes to.
The Italian word for piano
operating into Castilian
came with the keys to
An instrument that is a
piece of furniture
jumping with its own burden
upon the eardrum.
Now in rhythms of 110th Street.
the fingers of Noro Morales
falling on the keyboard
like the prints of Buddha.
In between the brass and
the timbas a pair of maracas
take off for the moon,
six hundred centipedes
crawl toward the foundation
of a crater where a whole
civilization of birds and cats
in the form of jinns
are dancing mambo.

In other realms the Harptones
deepened the echoes,
A ballad grind of jersey with
mohair,
Trio Los Pancho's lyrics melting
northern snow.
1946 Live at Manhattan Center
Noro's band of glitter shines,

crystal tingling of voices
with the sun for tongue
Early New York tropics
still dreaming of Arawak rivers.

Trains roaring Third Avenue El
cha cha cha,
East to West side
Sauté under orange lights
a stage with horses dressed
in black tuxedos,
Except Noro Morales
who was blasting a red jacket
with silk lapel.
The set of kitsch decors,
fake palm fronds
Background mural of campesinos
with straw hats,
Pineapples the size of
conga drums.
January cold hawk wind
still the rumba inside
Melts the ice in the highball
glasses.

111th Street mulatas
dancing with velvet dresses,
Bare backs of evening gowns.
Papayas and batatas
guanábanas jumping all around,
Tropical vista re-created
through dance steps.
Movement in the matrix of images,
island organization
The Caribes coming to eat you.

Noro breaks the scale down
do-re-mi-fa and continues down
sound to the far extreme of

the keys,
The body separating into
components,
Calves   legs   shoulders
bosoms   hips   waist,
Each as if a separate God,
Noro solos a prayer
for the joints,
Scattered within the phrases
of the "Cubanchero"
Knees depart through horns
bosoms through trombones,
hips migrate to Havana,
Waist goes spiraling toward
the south pole.

Out of space rotation
the sensation of the clave
meter in the Vivaldi pianola.
Italian columns
from between which Sabu
throws down cocos from his palms.
Figurines in frenzy marking
elegant timing form.
Spin your eyes in my arms.
Noro recognizes only rhythm
climbing Manhattan Center
walls falling like ripe fruit.
In the Hudson and East Rivers
A zillion fish swim toward
the Caribbean Sea,
Against all currents of habitat.
The dance floor is calling out:
Auxilio.

PEDRO SALINAS

Ever it was for you to write this way,
a chance of person, stars, architecture,
Those very castles (Castillo) of your
Spain
Its capital city Madrid, is it from *madrigal,*
breaths of short love verses,
Where light first entered your eyes.
Dissolving during Franco's antipoetics
toward the new world,
To contemplate the brighter light
to see everything much clearer,
Pores and sharp edges,
a face is more face, colors have more
juice and edge
The boundary where content ends
and the air begins
A piercing line of fine contours.

Through the hallways of Johns Hopkins
you exposed pearls to the barbaris,
taking your time with the Spanish
habit of salutation,
making ceremony of everyday moments.
Finally the Caribbean visual spectacular,
to see the sea
The clouds that move like thoughts,
the laughter at night,
The windows call out names,
the carpet into the sea,
the sand at your feet
"With green curves, with lazy foam,
light is the primordial artist."
Opens the marine world of the
tropics,
Letters like shells that the
waves bring,

A sea horse galloped through
his ears,
Nymphs of interior foam
walked out of the waves,
Syllables to repose upon
hammocks as original flesh.
Remembrance of Nereida's
water muses,
Her Yemaya dancers
flying upon the wings of rum,
Bailarinas in a blue mirror.

Did he go to the mouth of
el Río Grande de Loiza,
To Julia's sensual caresses
in the aurora of arms
Tree branch fingers pouring
through her hair,
Or to pre-Columbian gestures
made by spontaneous mestizo
esqueletos of timeless merging,
At river banks with gourds,
in madrigueras of subtle shadows
into caves where hands etched symbolic
iguanas bats
coming out at night
to jump over stars.

Out of the water came 1001
things,
Marble and scarves, chests full
of Castilian memoirs, guitars,
Paella spoons, berets
A camera reposed on a
giant shell,
Each photo another variation
deep in the night dreaming
the sea meditation,
Certain creatures and colors

for which there is no name,
Seeing from that other land
that the Indian ocean,
The Mediterranean, the Atlantic,
Red Sea,
are all united in the pupil.
Out there this blue sky
makes thought so pale,
Foam through a mile of curve,
the depth comes closer
to offer beams of light that dance
over the water,
This bride of liquid that has
eaten my eyes,
Upon her float these isles
of jade,
Girls in warm air dressing
slowly no rush Venus lips.
What makes these waves take
motion?
Angels that insist,
saltwater that cleans,
No wonder: Everything
more clear.

Salinas gave us the deeper
caverns of love poems,
Taking note of unformed gestures
invisible tremors of desire.
Not Neruda's twenty poems . . .
seashells of the shore
for Viña del Mar hullabaloo
rockeros,
Salinas abysmal lament
scrapes below the floor,
Searching for the forest
that abandoned the desert,
The sand rising from the
bowels reclaiming the pure

Rose,
The one that wants no other
thing than to be,
A clarity that knows the fragrance,
blueprint for the form.
His poetry of so many windows
meditating the blue vast reflection
of the sea above in the sky,
where flower stars grow
within aquatic gardens.
The waves still come to his feet
resting in San Juan,
Pointing toward the sea
Contemplated.

LA VIRGEN DE LA MONSERRATE
—to Iris Jackson

Cathedrals are wombs
trespassed by obelisk tree
of the cross,
erect pinching the hair
of the cave entrance, crevice,
Mountain interiors where
echoes create tremolos.
Hard-shell river crabs and reptiles
Twinkling the necklace of the bird.
Hidden in the Catalán mount
dark within dark,
Subconscious of stone,
rivers continue beneath the earth,
the stream inside the grotto
Shrimp grabbing what they can.
Bats fly through her ears as
she listens to slices of sun light,
attentive to atmospheric waves,
In trance/lation.
Sitting upon her throne
she has heard the songs made
by iron ore core of soiled mouth,
So purple and nasty.
So warm and nourishing
she sings to the child
on her lap
Next to the circular globe
spinning.

She sat in a cave for centuries,
when they tried to evict her
from her deep serenity,
She became as heavy as the earth,
they had to leave her
ebony whisper submerged
within the negritude of the grotto.

From her invisible radiation
she projected to all the windows
of Barcelona
Her sight reaching south to be
born in so many nymphs,
She took a ship to France,
in Marseilles she was hailed.
Isis of a blue awakening
Throughout the Mediterranean
the children of her darkness
The new moon eyelid of
Fishermen's horizons.
The child on her lap
is humankind,
(that sleep of gold)
The eye that sees in the night
Hidden
Still statuette
through the centuries: Unmoved
Come swords and cannons
and kingdoms falling:
Serenity within the womb.

In a small Puerto Rican town,
she came into the realm of sight.
Projected herself from the Catalán
distance of her interior,
To wave like our flag in Hormigueros,
under a mango tree,
next to a guava bushel,
under mameys hanging,
Became a batida malt,
guanábana juice,
Poured out of a coconut.
Her dark mahogany sculpture,
a guayacán tree rooted
in Angel breath,
Smiling cinnamon cheeks.
Incarnation of Caguana

Taina–Mora
Walking the streets.
She was seen so brilliant
Obsidian crystal.
Every September comes
her calendar,
In a procession upon shoulders.
The old people come out,
you stand near them when she
passes,
You feel something in the air,
hair rises abdominal butterflies
The people moving with candles,
like a snake of diamonds
the street ascends the parade
from a distance approaches a
door within the sky that touches
the street summit.
Later in the Patronales feast
there are Monserrates everywhere
pushing through the streets
like sizzling sparkling flesh.

CABEZA DE VACA
—*for Peter Rabbit*

Cabeza de Vaca took a stroll
to end all marathons.
Just about put a lid on the subject.
Through jungle and mesa,
tundra, mountains and rivers.
Bare-ass down ravines
keeping eye on peekaboo rattlesnakes.
Left his wine aging in Jerez,
No matter if hooligans from Cádiz
found it and drank it all.
From the Mississippi he
surrealed the Guadalquivir,
Dream travels of chimera mirages.
Bush pebble and stone.
Gophers prairie dogs trail of lost
men.
His feet in the last of the Cordoban
cowhide boots.
Starlit nights
de Vaca tossing and turning
A pinhead in the Nuevo Mexico
horizon.
Where was the loco going?
eyesight was a language,
The next day more sun to hide from.
But forward like an elephant
whose ass has been set on fire.

A stomp through virgin soil,
Andalusian marble for memory,
clowns and buffoons with the smells
of wayward ships.
Chants of Sevilla's deep song
in the circle dance of Taos Pueblo,
Shouts of Olé floating upon the Colorado River.

68

Eating buffalo stew,
through the same tongue
of olive oil.
Cabeza at the head of a posse of
Spaniards,
Covered in skins or naked.
Shedding their flesh
disappearing in the new horizon,
Entering teepees and mud huts,
peyote cactus singing through
their Catholic liturgy,
Footing through Texas eternity,
Pictures of the Roman aqueduct of
Segovia
appearing through waterless trails
of baked earth,
He saw the horizon get filled with
Saint James,
His ankles praying to the sounds
of new trees,
Hoping to step upon their names.

Conceive the motion:
Let's say you start footing in Miami Beach,
and arrived in Mexico City's Zócalo plaza,
Cabeza got Marco Polo's shoes where he left them
and tore Iberian ass,
Eating the stars that fell down as grapes,
immersed in never-before-tasted berries.
Transparent through arrows,
detours of tomahawks,
immune from poisonous herbs.
His castile became the arboreal kingdom.
Streams were his fountains
to so many forks in the road,
Fragrances that he read like signs,
hovering condors drawing in the
vast native sky,
Mountain peak smoke words

cow skulls hanging from trees
were his medieval books.
A suction took him forward,
through the maya of discovery.
As he traversed
he disappeared.
Losing all sense of his identity,
he descended into a sauna,
a native sweat lodge, kiva
Men and woman dressed like
butterfly wings elevating
from the humid fermentation of
La madre que los parió.

RICARDO RAY Y BOBBY CRUZ

When I was young goblins
tried to steal my spring,
monsters drying the flowers of
my thoughts. Beasts loose through
the delicate birth of rhythmic
awareness.
Yet many fragrances followed
my steps of dance.
Up on the roof the Empire State
Building held maracas,
The Chrysler Building played
bongos.
The first job I had
the first paycheck I got
I bought a portable radio,
to keep me zounded in my nights
of walks.
Sometimes groups of us
boys and girls,
Would weave through the tangle
of the streets,
Liquefy through the projects
to appear on the other side,
the Park,
Where the river played its tune,
watching the cannabis flow
along with the dark current.
The radio tuned to Symphony Sid
which in those years was
like Latin Jazz
One after the other
Cuba and New Orleans,
Wees was like mango trees
in tropical blues,
Walking what would be memoirs
and paintings.

From the river's edge
Brooklyn's megalopolis electric jumps.

Ricardo Ray more than fire
on the keyboard,
Was an acrobat flying on the
trapeze.
Swinging through the edifices
of a zillion light windows.
In the river park swirls of wind
coming out of the boom box,
Making musical frames
that could hang at
The Museum of Modern Art.
The Brooklyn Bridge was his
keyboard,
An overpass to protect
from the lava meltdown
Reddish clave below the bongos,
and the vegetative scratch of
the gourd,
The trumpets chemical into sharp
C's,
Like sound running in all directions,
a frenzy exploding into chorus.
Coro.
Yenyere.
Down the stairs the white keys
up to the roof the azabache marble,
vanilla and chocolate calling for sugar.
Same time Bobby Cruz is bringing
down the saints,
Cabio-sili yare Shango.
Pitches of Italian soprano
through migratory tamarindo.

Wees walks in the twilight
of teeny bop,
The way we strode

like the precious Manhattans
Algonquin steps
We retrace their shadows
and shared their night.

Bobby Cruz appears in a canoe
paddling the long pipes and feathers.
The clear water the bush of the banks
and the rocks becoming again,
The singer's face receives a splash
of notes from Ricardo's fingers.
His wooden face
a sculpture begun in Ghana
that jumped out of the Orinoco.

JORGE LUIS BORGES

Early he felt
what he would see in the future,
The arithmetic of the letters,
In the audio mandala of his house
where he took narrative as a wife.
A story always inside another
older than the wind,
A saga of the first exposures,
finally we don't see the words,
Images of speculation,
A map of Tango whore bars
port of call chulo guitars
Good Airs of shuffling feet,
black dresses, purple skirts
tight against the figurine,
Buenos Aires portal fresh.

Wind weaves through the arabesque
Balconies
youthful Seville water.
Moving like a stream of air
Horizontal, vertical colors
Incomprehensible infinity
Where are we amongst the
grains of sand?
Are we in some other where?
Who it is I is?
The book of sand I read
Upon an island beach.
Each grain another tale.

Taking off Darío's embroidered
Jacket
For a word that steps on color
tone of actual events
Nothing else in the way of the

Observatory.
A street cat is an elegant prince,
Who carries a Toledo sword,
Reflecting tired minds
Who think in terms of psychos.
His stories saw the screen alight
With the dance of breasts
Offering the milk of language,
Beauty the sight of knowledge,
saints and goddesses descending
upon the pen.
The first poets the hunters
by starlight
                    Piercing the wind
Writing with spears into
The moving shadows.

Borges folding the memoirs
Of his retinas,
The history of light,
Brings through the corridors
Our local foreign fancies,
Interglobal folk loom.
Che sitting in the corner bar,
The camera descends from the boats
To the street accordion,
The mustache, the hat
Carlos Gardel at the southern tip
of the language,
They say a Frenchman that
vitrols out of the Rio Plantense,
the tempo of the Habanera,
Musicians with black berets
symbol the Tango
In the way they drink
In the way they fight,
in the lovers' fierce language,
Our conversations of duality,
two cocks cross through sight,

Two men walk toward Palermo
Mother–of–pearl handled Derringers.

What night of the seven
we are relaxed
Amidst texts that have become
chairs
A leather-covered book
14-karat-gold letters illume
the castle's gates.

Borges with his London tweed,
Quixote of our America,
taste the tongue from Mexico
to Patagonia.
In a Byblios chamber of papyrus
a door opens
Onto a guest who strolls
through a garden.
Borges visits the fading pictures
of himself sitting,
His hands clutching
the silver cane handle
with the head of a tiger,
it lectures through his mouth:
that the world is a poet's dream.

LA VIRGEN DE GUADALUPE
—to Elena Flores

She danced for the man
who was camouflaged with the name
Juan Diego.
She was covered with a blue shawl
full of stars,
Venus the brightest,
Eva of the night
present in the sky of Tepeyac
before there were human eyes.
Her laughter and weeping.
Her scent
Along with the copal
in the outskirts of Tenochtitlán,
Tonantzín mother of seeds
creator of forms,
Hieroglyphic signs of her intention
through the horizon becoming.
Her Nahuatl lips
teeth of enclosed pearls
From which so much moon exits.

Her commands carry the night
from Tijuana to Chiapas,
Panlenques wide edifices
when they were new had the
Color of white seashells,
visible from the serpent
snake ships.
Guadalupe's eyes fulgor of the
sun upon the pyramid walls.
Through the fields of cactus
maguey her hot Mama heat-
wave of fertilizing desire
through Sonora's desert chill.
She fought against cabarets

full of Malinche bitches.
She made scarlet roses
grow on the archbishop's
Black robe,
A garden sprang
as his peninsular eyes popped,
The mother earth gave
him evidence, but,
There are some sons of Puts
that neither the physical
nor the spirit can find
they gaze the
air like frozen statues.
La Morena flames through
them an opening
An ice melt.
From a blue robe she changes
into green earth,
A child holds her up.
That same child pushed
in a carriage in the valley of Fresno
Rain goddess manifests
every day.
In California she held my hands,
breezes swirl all around,
Hanging in the car's rearview
mirror
Images of her many forms.
Lupe each day you change
your face,
A carnival of Lupitas
holding up the sky.
An aura of perfumes out of
her skin,
Her slanted eyes
speak the longings of this
Sun's age.

DON QUIJOTE
—*to Judith Ortiz Cofer & William Luis*

We arrived in Alcalá de Henares
through the roads of cool air vineyards,
olive tree shadow coplas.
Cervantes might have been born here,
I rubbed a lamp
Found in the medieval university,
hoping the genie would help
in the search for his house,
its Visigoth decors upon an
enormous door.
Perhaps his belly button
would still be interned between
the pages of his picaresque novels.

But how to search for Cervantes
when the whole town was in siesta.
An almost golden copy of *Don Quijote*
sat in a closed bookstore window.
Spaniards were asleep
or chewing on ham.
A total collapse of civic duties,
rest, wine, an afternoon coitus.

At the university
cigarette smoke creates clouds
in the hallways,
as if all the books were on fire,
Taino tobacco burning up
the Age of Gold.

No Cervantes to be found
except in a portrait
Where his eyes followed
as you walked.
El Quijote is more spread out

than the map,
Was he with us when we entered
the castle of Ávila,
Santa Teresa's finger floating
in a jar,
Pointing to San Juan de la Cruz
Who we had seen on a side street,
his ink of Islamic motifs
Dancing the Christ of wonders,
were awakened by a strong café
Which we had with a yard of
bread.
We searched through the corridor
out to cobblestone streets
that lead to crosses
and Saints pointing upward.
We jump again in the carriage
on to Segovia where El Quijote
might have challenged the
Roman aqueduct to a duel
mistaking it for a beast.
His quill of so-much ridiculous
stain,
Not a rock was left without its
water,
Humanity was made to laugh at,
The Castle stones are harder
when they are placed,
The more Duke they are the
more delusive head,
Not a hat fits the globe of air.
His malice with a narration spell
perhaps not hell but purgatory
where he dwells.
Motion through the kingdoms
he wondered more Castile
than El Cid.

The fountain we saw in Toledo
was it made with Quijote's
lost teeth? In every fisticuffs
he lost thirteen.
Who would invent that mouth
with a bipolar head.
Always out of place
like creation itself.
The axis poles waving
drunker than a Spaniard.
Sancho Panza customary stupor
finding the strength to discredit,
he was the province itself,
sugar-coated proverbs,
The corner tavern,
street talk,
aphorisms of the ages,
Words of the wind.
Dulcinea before Lolita
Toboso is not fixed.
it appears in new geographies,
not land but air,
Judith felt it in Paterson, New Jersey
Luis with rumba Manhattan.

It came with gusts of speech,
a novel written with all the air
circumventing the Earth.
Evening of the mad lector
dusting the old chivalry books,
Damascus gold laid deep
into the base of Hebraic bazaar.
The angels of Castile
had already crossed the Atlantic,
their crosses in the form of swords.
Cide Hamete Benengeli
sent a fax to Argentina
Borges got it in his ageless
machine.

We could write elsewhere
our bodies in jail,
We look out of a North African
window toward the sea
Imagining a woman's
eyes burning a hole in the
Rock of Gibraltar,
A purple orchid balanced
on the curve of a scimitar.

Rocinante on wheels gallops
through want of stone
and surprise of bush,
Through valleys of morons,
with this gallant chin,
talk way ahead of the scenery,
looking for any balls of bulls,
Why . . . I'll get off this mule
and split any who in two
that contraries my score,
or that thinks in music more
delight than that which
I invent for horns to glow
upon gentlemen's heads high and low.

If Cervantes invented a unicorn
with wings
To fly over the Caribbean
he would have seen,
on a clear night,
the Antillean archipelago
sparkling like a diamond necklace
with the electric juice,
all the lights from Trinidad
to Jamaica
its trees and beaches
fruits and flowers
Its mulato soul,
So much carnival of pages,

Bays of unforgettable blues,
Women who are a thousand
eyes of Dulcinea,
Doroteas to throw away,
popular philosophers demonstrating that
Every theme has its madman.

Make the world what you are
Don Quijote de la Mancha
de Plátano.

Born 1126 Cordoba
but where and how.
I went looking asking the statues contemplating
the Almoravide wall which mother which wife
of your father. Your Romance blood. Your Berber bones.
Your Arab nose. But what will we gather from speculation
you were all parts and each difference eminent. Your family
of high balcony, garden flowers circulatory village, did you as
a child, play near the ruins of
the Medina Azahara, the Berbers in fitna had already
set it ablaze, did you take walks to stare at the one
thousand marble columns of the palace A medina built
there by Abdermann III for his beautiful wife Zohrah, witness
to the flower of al-Andalus Islam, the gem atop the gold.
Did you see the terraces go down the stairs. When did I
know about you when did I first hear your name saw it in
print in the Latin form Averroës stumbled upon Jorge Luis Borges
who was in search of you in the *kitab El Aleph* your name
was long like your knowledge a fountain of rhythmic water
the sway of it birds of love. It is precise scale of piercing thought
in clarity like water running through canals, one moment at an
instance, bringing out the light of the books shipped upon
camels' back and floated on caravels till they reached your hands
in Cordoba, these were the words of Aristotle translated into
Arabic there in the Baghdad of grandeur. What was your desk
like? Low upon the floor where you sat crossed-legged glass of tea
shelves with books planted horizontal desk matter marble
like a pearl at times ink stained, your son Abul Qasim Ahmad
comes into play a housemaid after him.
The house second story of tile flower patterns
of nature fired into the brilliant clay, outside orange tangerine
trees fragrance through the passages separating palm fronds
drooping the environment of lucid language, sometimes the
street vendors barking almonds or sweet pastries, eaten by
Plato, Aristotle, and other Greek visitors sitting across from you
upon the divan poetic. Explaining the revelation in the morning
    with the sun,

the miracle the verses in nature, asking the divine questions
late night by lantern, the position of the stars affects the mood
of the pen, men below the street speak in Amazigh language
of the Atlas Mountains in Africa, the Almoravides serious
glitter of the sword brings Almohades silver spades; through it all
divided between the Mosque and the philosophic flight, the
Greek content without its language upon the al-Andalus rug,
knowing the gentle nature of the men curious of everything that
makes sense,
aware of the lawyers taking the word to the letter, prompting
things at value of the face, forgetting life's possibilities the sounds
of the language suggesting further Guadalquivir flowing.
When Cordoba earth shook you were gone to Sevilla,
came back to city beloved to find the buildings crooked, the sand
of the Sahara that fell from the sandals of the recently arrived.
Comparing the two vaiven Andalusia/Africa north, the texture
of the sky. Wondered as always about the people and what they
could comprehend, saw them in layers like geologic stratas, each
function unique looking to become as they must to abandon the
beast. The circle you were in the doctor Ibn Tufayl who carried
the ceremony of loneliness from Ibn Sina the other doctor from
Persia, wrote his novel of a boy lost island isolation discovers
the gifts of Allah by natural search still we all need cities
the libraries of the generations, the text gets passed down, beyond
the parchment, the silence of the moon upon the papyrus,
you made comment upon such antiquity expanded lucidity
upon the prophecy, the letters of the algebra of distance, it
came here through someone, enough we are eye and ear, aroma
and skin, some can achieve the language while others need
the theatrics of the ceremony, with your sandals within the
two chambers, bringing dream to light of reason. And
for what concern you left for the town of Lucena was it exile
or the simple stepping upon your jellaba; there you dwelled
in the library of Maimonides the Jewish wizard who wrote
in Arabic, did you exchange monotheistic phrases the letters
Semitic curves and hooks from right to left from east to west
following print to the sun fall, with you all in the rooms rewriting
things turning them inside out, listening to them upside down.
The botany of your garden in the climate you shine the mestizo

of the streets, the Spanish forming brand-new rawhide
Berber, Moroccan Arabiya. The auburn hair romano hispano
in the mosque Aljama de Cordoba when the walls were white outside
fresh air inside musk fragrance folded in prayer alongside Yusef and
Ya'qub in the manuscript fingers soft coppice, covers leather, scrolls,
passage of finger and palm through grain of places,
reading is the past present. Now they say they cannot find your books
in Syria, the books that explained books, the words coherent revealing
incoherency. Your Spanish heart in Arabic, a universal Andaluz as
Juan Ramon Jiménez would have said, chaos out of your fingers
turns serene and breaks with the sun over the valley of Cordoba
reaching into the pure simplicity of light in the night.

MONGO SANTAMARIA

Growing with rhythm in the city of Manhattan,
Latin flavor African, always the trains and the buses,
the sounds of play and talk, the walkers, whether dancers
or not people always walkers in the cold winter and in
the summer somewhere always remember the high
moments of the beats of Ramon Mongo Santamaria,
as if he and the cow or goat skin atop the wood of many
red Timbas were in the steel frame of buildings connected
all one to the other through vibration, sometimes eight
stories up into the cement a certain streetcorner
would have Caribbean sound, see it bunched up split
into forms of energy taken from the wind looking
like a Wilfredo Lam painting, like sudden urban Senegal
imagination or Bantu divination a wire shaking skeletons,
dancing on the cruelty of Portuguese boats, you would see
lines of dancers from antiquity, fertility vaccination followed
by circles. It was just his hands inspired that made so much
Literature—When I first saw him it was at the Village Gate of the
mid-sixties; in the man such quietude, a calm, gentleness
before opening the floodgates of beats, a phrasing, all drummers
were different you could tell who it was eyes closed,
Mongo's stories had more vocabulary, you could hear vibration
of the ceda wood or caoba the boards with the belly of rich milk
cows. We were seventeen in the Village Gate illegally, we
would break any law to be near the drums, at the time I
didn't dance so well I would see the girls Marias and Carmens
from the Bronx and Brooklyn and be frightened by their
beauty and perfume, as we were also startled by Mongo's
solos, when all the strings and the brass disappeared and they
left him scripting calligraphy to the ancestors, like fire
falling onto the wood of the stage burning through, Shango,
down onto Manhattan earth, a weight focus pounding,
the modernity of the nation destroyed, becomes all tribal
horse jump, forward, the steeples of the guaguanco tips
of trumpet saxophone, a piano snowing coconut sprinkling
rose water, around the whole place oxygen shortest,

we lift onto our feet to jump in case, spot red exit sign above
door possible through there was salvation,
at each turn a different proverb from his fingers, would not stop
slight breaks to pile further annihilation, we thought serious that
smoke far loneliness of Cuban palms, opener of paths as
cement and steel melted, we follow once again the Algonquin/Iroquois
geography of the island to the river turned into the Niger, where
along its trees we see hanging faces, we have no decision in
the movement the dance is on command, was what Mongo
doing slowly controlling bodies such a relative power to move,
to churn, like in "Oye Este Guanguanco" the music clave in reverse
Mongo popping his beats above the singing heads, TACUN TAB
TACUN TOK, dancers feel it between the legs, the tip of the shoe.
It's the only way I understand advance mathematics, the beats
make the ciphers fluid red fire, if you count twenty-two slaps
on the left drum and thirty-four on the one to his right, sum them
together realizing you heard them as tint, which is the flavor,
so hard his hands make the soft build-up of shades to make
pictures rise above the city of presence. Back during *Watermelon Man*
passing the Apollo Theater we see his name in big letters
half of the only high school in Harlem, Ben Franklin on 116th
cut class to hit the matinee, the movie what was it, come the
brilliant stagelight showtime, in the center of his sound was
blues and guanguanco and you couldn't find the border,
like everything raining, back then the Apollo had this stage where
the platform the band jamming suddenly came forward,
Sitting up close Mongo came toward me, afraid he
was going to slap me cross-head so close to the conga,
under the chairs the books were piled that day we saw
Mongo at the Apollo and never made it back to school.
Santa Maria.

Island Waves

"So looking through a map
of the islands, you see
rocks, history's hot
lies, rot
ing hulls, cannon
wheels, the suns
slums: if you hate
us. Jewels,
if there is delight
in your eyes.
The light
shimmers on the water,
the cunning
coral keeps it blue."

—KAMAU BRATHWAITE, *Islands*

"I had come all the way here from the sea,
Yet met the wave again between your arms
Where cliff and citadel—all verily
Dissolved within a sky of beacon forms—
Sea gardens lifted rainbow-wise through eyes
I found."

—HART CRANE
from "Key West and Bees of Paradise"

ISLAND WAVES

ISLAND WAVE I

The bodies are taking time serene
like rum being cured in barrels.
The same time of year
the same songs.
Stars drop into your black hair
as streams of white light.
Standing upon such little earth
we feel the pull of the sky.
Some mornings we wonder
if it is not up that we walk.
There must be something
in the depths of the caves,
Half a world of creatures
is down there,
Some nights there is a howling,
a hissing,
Other times a grumbling
a stomping
As if dinosaurs have been
awoken.
Could it be Caguana tired of
squatting in Utuado
Walking toward me,
with a simple cotton nagua
full of dark humid air?
Solar monotheist deity of
the Tainos
The disk the mirror of noon.
Flashes of light are seen in
the rivers
It is the flash appearances of the
Goddesses of water
Signaling out to the wombs,
contained and fulfilled

throughout the region.
Drunk coconuts are staggering
zigzagging through the loud
voices of bored routine.
In tune more to the silence
listen a stone has walked
to my door,
It is Caguana thirsty with many
roots hanging from her mineral.
She squats into the mouth
of my words.

ISLAND WAVES 2

Santurce is like the Maghreb
in the Caribbean,
The peoples could exchange places
as you will see they are the same faces.
The Caribbean of exposure,
no jellabas or caftans covering curves,
This is the stream of the Orinoco,
nudity like Brazilians in Carnival.
Camels parked at La Plaza del Mercado,
Mercado,
Salsa Fest. In Marrakech medina.
In both spaces bodies are rattling
like nervous twitches,
An endless parade of legs,
a bubbling that climbs walls.
Passion fruit juice and mint
tea exchange glasses.
The coastal fish sees eye to eye.
As if in the time of al-Andaluz Spain
the Guadalquivir merged with
the river Niger.
Alcapurrias for the fishermen
of Casablanca.
The night brings our sharp distance,
Santurce disappears as if the
darkness was a fire,

Figures scurry to their enclosures.
In the Maghreb streets are like
public manifestations,
Throngs walking randomly
in close proximity,
The Cafés are percolating,
cawah wiring through the
Nerves of rug designs
speaking in colors.
Santurce sits with its bedlam,
an invisible whip puts it to
sleep.
That's why going home
is finding a sofa for the memory,
North Africa,
the Caribbean
Confused.

ISLAND WAVE 3

Between the lips the cheeks and the eyes
is the map of the world,
Civilizations in miniature her smile,
lips of Senegal, buttocks of native freedom.
Berber eyes from the Atlas Mountains
The coasts all touch her face,
her ears are boats,
The hills of her breasts
languages of so much suck,
Roman faces that sing guarachas,
in our hands it is like a fruit
Seeds and sweetness
Pulp in reproduction,
anything can come out of anything,
Island riverbeds
Through which so many seamen
have come,
Sailing between the legs
of the crescent bay.

TRICOFERO

Hair of my Father

to Severo Merced Cruz, Papá
October 10 1923–June 23rd 2005

My father had no illusions or imagination,
he was in actual reality
hard and unforgiving,
What the world of the mountain gave him
not to expect anything,
Simple love or tenderness
such a luxury as foreign as the
cold snow of northern latitudes.
People with sharp eye staring
the mountain houses were made of wood,
only thing to do was leave
or become an owl posted upon night tree,
looking at the shadows of hopeless skeletons.
Down toward the valley he saw the
lights of the town,
Slow he started walking, it was so remote
and alien,
down there getting there. When he was young
he had to descend or not go to school,
staying with relatives who located him
another mouth to feed,
did he sleep like a bat corner of a corner
hanging,
Dawn edging people's eyes open
still dark café aroma,
a breeze from the mountains guayaba mango
tobacco scents, it was 1936 everything was wood.
Memories of Bayamoncito mountain barrio
grim nights of insomnia,
a corn mush called funche
a lantern called quinqué roosters so important,

the first motion of sky illumination they celebrate,
later they sing to the moon night.

The whole Caribbean screams in his hair,
father's bones with the scares of the chains
from his ribs hung whips of Cordoba leather.
These mountain families were the outlaws
of the outlaws, they hid from the fugitives,
in the enclave at the end of the world,
parts of gadgets and love hints
in the necessity of the sunlight barely visible,
twisted bent warped, melted full of bacteria.
What glimpses do I have of him picking
the memories of his own father off the
trees that gave no fruit just bare within the
drought of responsibility.
He was a mulatto with the skin of a reptile
He told me once of his cold blood before he
drank a scorching cup of tea,
His snake tongue like nothing.
He told me too that he was not sure
of the date of his birth
They brought me down the mountain
into the town and registered me there
that day he was one and a half in his mother's hands,
my grandmother could not read she told another
Illiterate woman and together they misspelled his name,
Everything settled in nebulous disorder.
My grandfather a shadow without body
who cared for no one,
I don't know if they once heard him whispering
sweet things to the calabaza vines to
encourage their growth.
The inland small enclaves made lots
of men like that,
Maximo had many women with all of
them children,
where my father and his brothers lived
was just one unit going down the mountain

the main wife in the big house
was his mother's cousin,
they had to be bitches to each other,
never spoke to one another all of existence,
retinas of sharp chaveta curved tobacco knives.
Within my father the scar was silence
anger and a rude discipline.
When I went with him to Bayamoncito
I could still hear his ancestor's bones
dancing under the ground,
it was past midday the sun opening
through the trees down the winding road,
the mosquitoes avoided his lizard skin,
his cured leather;
nothing went into him
nothing came out.

But I watched him closely and found
where he was hiding,
there he was like crying a little boy in my arms
scared of the crustacean horrors of the river,
the giant river crabs of indifference,
the mindless shrimp of down pull flow,
embarrassed at the way people looked
at him in the shadows over the shoulder,
such thirst he had for tenderness,
I saw through the shell
the veil pulled over his wounded soul,
saw how he offered me what was never
given to him,
a labor of vigilance that never came to an
end.
All creatures that approached he mistrusted,
knew they just wanted resources without justification,
moving colors melting jagged teeth toward one,
marauders sharp like mechanical cubism
stink of vampire wings, hungry falcons
over the desolate terrain.
The imposition of the imprudent

heavy upon our heart tissues like water
surrounding,
till liquid chokes the organ of thought amor
which was a weapon for him,
cannons coming out of the medieval
cement.

We forgive them cruel humanity
that we imagine not to think it.

If you want illusions and tenderness
go watch Walt Disney cartoons,
but if you want to see the true face of humanity
talk to my father Severo
the truth of the actual devil with a tail
fuming mouth fire,
gray scaly skin sitting in the kitchen.
He always told me society is a bunch of thieves,
the seeds we planted eaten by animals,
Goats are everywhere hungry
with their horns protruding into the sun.
Cabrones

Always plant three seeds into the earth,
I asked him why,
He said:
One is for the neighbor,
one is for you
and the other one is for the thief.

So it was the last years we spent them going up
the finca the country land he had
We would do anything just to be together,
one time we dragged shovels and all the
equipment needed to mix cement
up to a mountain peak
and in the middle of the jungle we made
a cement column
it took us two weeks;

Now I know the reason why,
we just wanted to be together
in the mountain, amid the trees
and the birds and the butterflies
Away from people away from society,
today I have seen another reason
the birds use it as a resting post
before flying on to more sky.

Up there together we spent the years
slashing away with our machetes,
we cleared a whole mountain of shrub
for no proposal in the landscape sight,
just harmony working the earth,
feeling the land under the sun with
our straw sombreros pointed,
My father had more work power than me
he had an insistence that I painted
with imaginative flights affecting this
way my stamina.
Once we were out there when a downpour
of rain came down
thick and rich wetness,
We had to cover ourselves with
big banana leaves
Into our eyes we look together
and we laugh at the predicament,
I saw him red and aboriginal
I saw him like a mask from Ghana
So close to me scent and pores,
then a flash back in time:
Saw myself in New York
after his separation from my mother,
he found a furnished room on St. Mark's Place
Lower Manhattan close to where I lived,
He'd take me there weekends
we slept together,
He made me read to him in Spanish and
English,

He had this dictionary called
Magnus: Diccionario Inglés Castellano
Editorial Sopena Argentina
its publication date 1950,
we searched for words I'd never heard of.
Today I still have that dictionary the very one
we held in our hands in a cinema now gone
that epoch of hard times New York,
Papi went from job to job,
drove a bus, worked for the post office,
once he showed up with an old Packard
that looked like a frog,
We took trips in it to Spanish Harlem
101st Street to visit relatives,
those pictures are with me now in my fingers,
Sundays he'd pick me up in the mornings
to take me to church,
a Methodist church a block away,
as he was always taking me off the streets
concerned with the dangers that lurked there.

He had the insight to take me to
the 1964 World's Fair in Queens,
he knew it was magic,
my friend Andrew came
a blond German kid from my block,
the planetarium stars beheld the future cars,
it was all future that we presenced,
my father with his past of wooden houses
bamboo and tropical insect sounds,
a vacuum within him immense.
Remember that the Mormons
had a kiosk and the man speaking Godly
my father always religious
brought a Mormon Bible.
The train coming back from the future
he looked at the words,
present in the chaos of his life,
now in the hallelujah of God's house

his sight chills within my writing palms.

I had seen my father cry in secret
many times,
migration mixed with personal torment,
history and life together hurt.
Always my father Papá
never my friend
As it is a lot more to be a father,
never he liked for me to call him Severo
always Papí,
Always requested a bendición from me,
Dios lo bendiga
He never stopped or derailed from that
mission.

Our struggle in the final years:
to recuperate lost time,
the years of immense distances,
holes of our lost lives.

Where does time go,
I ask myself, sitting in the funeral
car his body in the coffin in the back,
I am the only one who rode with him,
The only one who carried his body
back to Aguas Buenas,
the road and the mountains a bird's
eye view of his life.

I buried his body like a seed into the
ground,
sensing his hair will sprout in another dimension
as guayaba fruit,
scent returns to Allah.
Through the opening of caves,
Dios who selects children and parents,
deep inside the sperm dance.

How deep the sky blue was when
we arrived into the cemetery,
when the protocols of flower and song
were over,
carrying the coffin toward the tomb
rain clouds gathered
quickly a rain shower of tears came down,
it was like wet light under the dream
this creator not man nor woman
not human
cold indifference forgiving abundance,
severe my father Severo told me.
When we settled his coffin into the
rectangular space of the tomb
I looked above toward the mountains of
his birth saw him taking my sister's
hands
together they walked into the eye of the
sun.

THE TOWN IN THE MOUNTAIN

Street dogs
are the owners of the darkness
of the town.
They live off the waste of
the civilized,
They have their own mayor
and administer their own laws.
They write letters to the frogs,
they call cats up on the telephone.
They occupy all the silence that
has been abandoned.
Their breath is a form of sight.
They take turns with the bitches
who become pregnant from a few
within the same placenta.
The barks seem to come
from the trees.
Out there in the distance
near the foot of the mountains,
from the last streets,
They poeticize the moon
invite her to come down
to share some bone.
They incorporate into your
nightly toss and turn,
barks of pillow turns within
dim obscurity.
Jumping from one dream to another,
an eye opens to the shadows
and the forms,
We sit momentarily to think what
it is all about,
Allah we whisper.
Returning to the darkness of
the stupor,

We dream the details of animal
interiors,
In photographic clarity,
while street dogs
just smell and mount ass.

BLUE BOAT

From the streets people were
jumping into passing clouds,
What I wanted to say was
that the street was like a glass
of water into which an effervescent
Tablet had been dropped
creating streams of upward
rising bubbles.
In order to hear you must stroll
with the silence that helps
you see better,
Look at what I am telling you
that words can be seen,
The people opening their windows
each gives me some details,
A story I once heard,
rhythmic songs.
How a mirror broke one time
says it was with thoughts,
pushing into the air,
just like you are in a thread of hair,
or a drop of sweat,
Composers of little bottles.
Water is everywhere what cleans
down the stairs onto the sidewalk,
a steam rises with the memory
of frog's breath.
Clean yourself. Ablutions before
you leave the house before you
enter the gates of praying musk.
Even in January cold your eyes
are hot
With the spirit of the land
of papaya,
In July the northern regions warm up
and you skip within your element,

I've seen girls skipping through New York
as if they were in Jajuya or el Cibao,
Kneecaps like headlights,
producing hurricanes with the flapping
of their dresses,
Turning to look at the storm
We behold their little
buttocks,
their skinny legs.

Early in the morning the massive
day is before us,
The noise is gathering for its
performance,
There is a roar in 1969 Manhattan,
my feet begin to laugh through
the streets,
Throngs of people who have invented
themselves,
All swirling upward like a Mister
Softee cone on its way to heaven
Upon a blue boat
On a blue boat of hop hips
On a blue boat of skulls,
Ship a hoe with a mambo
of a thousand trumpets
And 400 timbales
for the eight hands of Tito Puente.
It is the secret destiny of the
navigator,
Who sits at the helm,
of the blue boat that is today.

HAIKUS

Tropical fading,
new land auburn trees dance just
like the girls back home.

At the grocery
apple falls from man's left hand—
bending—head hits edge.

Ah, is it silk gown,
even the worms could be food,
No, imitation.

I look upon tree—
grapes hanging all over it,
the eyes of women.

Brown hands red nails sway,
white dress white hands red nails wave,
black hands, nails, white dress.

City News 1

Wallet in pocket
Money stuffed like burrito
Look! gone, man slices wind.

City News 2

Into self-service
elevator he goes smooth
Bang! now stuck he hums.

City News 3

All morning he heard
screwdriver making hall sounds
Mailbox! now he thinks.

Textile

She wear the pants red-
dish and tight what is under
neath nature hills fly.

Iota

A roach from Colom-
bia has enough legs and
walks the ocean back.

HANDS

My hands reach out of the boat,
to touch the water that is more than land.
Coastal flows, fish and marisco
saltine motion, olive hands, black eyes
reproduce, bread rising.
The Mediterranean—the Caribbean waves
of the same wetness,
different departures corresponding arrivals,
Five hundred years an instant upon the sand,
a few grains in the cosmos of time.
We have made ourselves out of the water,
from fish to jail birds escape from dungeons,
priests of splintered crosses,
a tongue licking the horizon.
Water and its endless burn,
those who have walked upon it,
those who have set it on fire.
My hands have come out of the caves,
like midnight vampires stretching out
as bats, arms of limestone bones.
Flesh of red clay dripping with insects.
A darkness of original air
its fingers of sacred pictographs.
Its wrist of broken bone
recomposed for further chiseling.
I have seen hands that engrave shells,
that weave hammocks,
Flesh of red clay rolling cigars,
later upon the balcony smoking.
Have you taken a
good look at your hands,
Tambourine hands,
guitar string plucking hands,
All hands of hidden touch desire,
Old hands that have not wrinkled,
pressing against the cotton,

music rush through flesh and nerves,
Touching silk what is skin,
what is fabric.
Hands that have built adobes
hands that have risen teepees,
Bohío building hands when the mountains
spoke native sweet.
Hands forming corn surrullos,
farming canucos.
Touching lip hands,
kissing dark skin hands.
Medina hands of our
first communities,
Mint leaf hands,
Hands of Baghdad physicians
pointing through books of organs,
Fingers like branches coming out
of the soil of your palms.
Granada red tile roof
laying hands,
Hands of Cordoba leather artisans.
Tangiers hands full of rings.
Cádiz, Huelva, Palos hands of sailors
tying rope, sailing hands.
Hands of curanderas.
Old ladies, hands of Doña Isabela,
her wax candle hands.
Her other hands invisible helpers,
the powerful hand,
In the picture the five fingers,
blood in the palm.
Forgiving hands, and striking hands.
Restless hands, frenzied hands.
Quick loose hands of slaps.
Hands of no repentance,
hands where Satanás sleeps and
keeps a playground.
Out of the boats many hands
of thieves,

Hands that speak disappeared gold.
Callous hands of cruel conquest,
hands that held the swords.
Entire Mars and Venus of hands,
love and war,
Hands that caress the night,
hands of Toledo knives.
Folded hands of rocking chair gossip
in San Carlos churning.
Castanet hands of flamenco women
rhythms working on a route to paradise.
Hands of bolero sleeves painted
by El Greco.
Parrots upon foreign hands
learn quickly new words.
The last being to say *love* in
Arawak was a parrot posed
upon mestizo hands.
Hands that pull the rope that
makes the church bells resound,
Hands that climb to the tower
of the minaret and verse
the morning prayer.
Hands of celibate priests jerking
through the night,
Nun hands of steady vibrato.
The conquest turned Castilian
hands dark,
Now copper hands play new
trobas,
Now black hands are our grandfathers,
Bantu fingers, Yoruba knuckles.
Coastal hands that have swum
the rivers inland.
African hands of Berber commerce,
gold traders,
Handling up from Timbuktu,
Sahara hands we are when we clap it
or don't know it.

The shape of the hand
the shape of the map.
Hands that have paddled out of the Orinoco,
red hands, moving hands,
Toasted hands of bongo slaps,
Ox whipping hands with wagons
full of cane,
Hands frenzy on goatskin drum.
Marimba playing hands
making birds resound out of wood,
Tortilla slapping hands,
pyramid building hands,
Cemi shaping hands,
fingers that mold stone.
swift hands, sleigh hands.
Tarot card hands
the Moon of the Enchantress
The Magician on the shore of Tangiers.
Hands with eyes
hands with noses
Hands that walk like feet.
Hands that remember
they were the tips of wings.
Garment District hands of 1958
mothers weaving the thread,
Hands of mountain picking herbs,
yerba bruja hands
Rompe saraguey, mejorana,
in fingers that pray by caves
and rivers they say on full
moon nights.
Chocolate melting hands,
Vianda for pasteles grating hands.
Medium hands of electricity.
Picture sending hands,
upon you healing hands.
The hand of Fatima halting evil
at the doors.
Fishermen's hands netting the

whole Caribbean.
Unknowing hands
unwanting hands.
Fake hands
No hands.
Patato's hands
Houdini's hands
Rubalcaba's piano hands.
Blessed cooks of bacalao hands.
Tito Puente hands,
Sammy Sosa hands.
Native hands that were trees,
Iberian hands of crucifix swords.
North African hands
of henna geometries,
Flowers climbing from the
knuckles.
Hands that made knots on the boats,
hands that turned trees into canoes.
Hands that jumped out of the sea,
Sea that has jumped out of the hands.
Hands that will jump back
into the sea.
HANDS / MANOS.

STILL LIFE
—*for Elizam Escobar*

Henry Moore runs his thumb
through the profile of el Yunque's
mountain range.
Two guanábanas bounce down
through an inclination
obeying the law of gravity.
Such ovals full of coconut water
weight of the dark nipples with
hazelnut rings like Saturn.
They pause when they reach the
sand of Luguillo for Botero's
index finger to take measure
of the highest mountain range
of the forest.
From a window the coconut grove
paints itself above the buttocks
of Blasina being carried off by Satan,
into the grease of Piñones,
kiosk after kiosk of burning corn
The plaintain coast of voltage
mulatez.
Later she will buff the bronze,
till she drops the curtain to expose
fools.
Jump from the frame
onto the sofa that belongs to a cat
preying upon the woman folded,
Imagining the whole island.
Amazona eating a fruit
The guava of Hesperides,
mountain fat legs,
Cuba's Cárdenas is back from Paris
caressing black stone near ceiba trees,
Like playing mineral drums,
Congolese spirals of marble

dancing to Siboney flutes,
One of his rocks has eyes
that can see the star Sirius
it was also in the pupils of
the Dogan tribe,
In the Africa without telescopes
they had their eyes upon
the dog of the sky.
His sculpture of wood,
Caoba that has come out
of the sun.

Blasina is now in the sea,
her waist the shape of Pablo Cassals's
Cello,
The wet guayacán cheeks,
Her ears made of leaves.
A thousand trees are in the water.
She dries herself and reposes
in the frame of *Interludio*
A Persian cat at her feet.
She stares through an open door
of a Piñones bar,
Unto faces floating like mamey,
pineapple lips,
The counter of the bar looks like
Juan Gris's
Guitar, Glasses and Bottle
a wooden grain that has lifted
the parquet floor,
As through a window
jumps the doors
In celebration.

The wrist veins of Diego Rivera
painting peasant feet,
Across a Mexico of revolution,
A Mexico in the movies of
mariachi singers.

The night comes from the depth
of the sea
Drops down onto the spine
of the mountain.
The plantain leaves look
like elephant ears
Being swallowed by bushy
bamboo.
Who is it that walks out of
the canvas?
The judges have been jailed
in the oil of the paint,
Exposed and frozen from
further movement,
from legislating the sentence

Escobar sees us from the
cells of his freedom,
Gives us the awareness
in form and color in
La Explanation
The mirror looking at us.
We are all captured in the
paws of a cat,
The two eyes looking
straight at us,
through the doors of
the Nation.

THE SIX POURED
—Para mi abuela Lea

In July Cagua's heat competes
with Death Valley,
A slow kind of roasting
with more moisture.
The plaza has a giant bird cage,
two Taino parrots captured
within.
They stare at you staring at them,
they are sure you have come
to exhibit yourselves.
There is a tall clock by
some benches
Gives you the time
and the faces of famous
islanders.
José Gautier Benítez is standing
in the center of the plaza,
His poetry of panoramas,
of Taina heroines,
Of flowers in the airy romance
of fragrance.
The taxis lined up with their
tired drivers one after the other
wasted by the sun's waves.
The water fountain puts us
anywhere in the Renaissance.

This town holds my grandmother
her eyes that saw another epoch
sewing dresses and cooking food
somewhere in a quiet street within.
I remember the last time I saw her,
in her aboriginal squat
Smoking a cigar.
She cooked goat stew for me

as I reposed recuperating
from a pulled molar,
Walking with her in the backyard
she yanked a leaf from some bushes,
Told me to put it where the wound of
the gum bled,
It put a stop to it.

Our embrace had been tears,
for I had not seen her in years
It was a miracle we were together.
Here I am to see you
as I said I would,
Overcoming the years of
geographic fragmentation.
It was in the valley of Caguas
that I said farewell,
Her hands forever handing me
medicinal herbs,
Stirring the pot of goat stew,
Forever in the focused
light of suns that have turned
to twilight.
Silence there is a memory,
I want to hear the way she looks
growing in my hands.
Silence the mountains,
Silent the lips of Caguax.

TRAVELING SIGNALS

These words have been given to
me by the road,
They have been fermenting through
bus windows
Swift intervals of shadows—street lights
sudden windows aperture domicile
a figure face a history,
like gifts of the motion.
The pictogram vocab of the letters
Shape them into your mouth,
these words are yours,
Wrap them in banana leaves,
Cook them in tangines,
mount them upon couscous.
Pierce them with shish kebab
skewers.
Savor them slow with the summit
sun,
To see the azabache print upon
the inner meat of the coconut
page,
Take them to your people of
bones,
Encantate upon the tomb,
meet there with your new
illusion,
Dine upon the marble,
Give a kiss that can be
felt by the past,
Place them upon trees
next to fruits,
Have the populous pick
them ripe.
Place them on boats
and drift them out to sea.
each time you say them

They should be as a kiss,
the commas and periods
like nails and screws
of the construction.
These words picked up
at border crossings,
Suitcases stuffed like
dictionaries.
Do the sounds of these words
have the howling and screeches
of the conquest?
The cocks of Europe
jumped upon the verdal virginity
of new land breasts,
Rising like mountains out of
liquid emerald.
They must've smelled the
fruit pulp in the Plaza Mina
of Cádiz.
How much of it taken
back in the sound of golden
letters
Romance tongue stung with
chili peppers spitfiring
new vocabularies,
Beyond the reach of
La Real Academia.

Hunchback from carrying so
much baggage onto
plane-boat-train-taxi-foot,
Journeys of aching backs,
swollen feet,
But always with flashes
momentary glimpses of
gestures souvenirs of the
safari.
From the action recreating
forbidden thoughts,

Cimarrones outlawed from terror,
hiding from the sophisticated city
behind the walls,
Out here are the birds
the mountain falcon,
The wild stream,
Down here I hide from
the north and rescue their
words from the cruelty of
their own pretension,
As I simultaneously deal
with homegrown avocados
And river shrimp
tumbling in the current against
their will with no knowledge
of habitat.
The places all come together
the races meet and the
features show all at once.
This Spanish of Spanish
where blasphemy is like
tenderness,
Boiling bile,
Pirates contraband the
coastal cities,
Tight faces trying to laugh
a kind of performance
grimace.
Like bits and pieces
floating waiting for a painter
to arrange it all,
With an eye for composition.
The boats still move through
the vein channels,
the hate we love
comes together,
chinga la chingada el chingao,
San Juan Bay like bosoms,
a vertical smile
taking so much ship.

Do with these words
what you wish,
These words are your
bride.
In some remote epoch
they belonged to others,
Place the accents where
you feel them,
Plant rows of letters
as if they were trees,
Borrowed speech
none of it belongs to us,
Stolen and recomposed
bodies,
The imperialism of art history.
Keep making the sounds
of creation,
Till we enter again
into the forest,
Flying from branch to branch.
making nests of
complete sovereignty
Under a full moon
that lets us see in
the dark.

THERE IS NOTHING BUT THIS

There is nothing but this
and this exactly is what it is?
It comes from this and goes to this.
All is this.
This is within this.
There is no other that is this
and such is the way it is spoken of,
This then is how it is
it is represented in this way,
For it is the way it is and
what else could it be.
Within the being of ares
it is the its of whats.
It is the whole silence maintained in sound,
it is the shape of octagons,
diamonds and stars, ovals, spirals
The corner circles of the imaginative sky.
Can it be other than this
reflected in the mirror of image sentiment,
This is the way it is
and it is that which it says that it is.

What else could this.
What else could that?

What has been said that it is
is what it is,
And nothing else is like it.
like this it is
What it is.
And it is here represented
by what has been verse-spoken
From within the shapes and forms,
imagine what you imagine.
In such a way that things are
they are then disposed to be.

Such a way it is that you paint
the Rock of Gibraltar for instance,
Surrounded by blue water,
notice why it is that it is,
Making your colors speak.
It was put there this way to sea
traveling to it when it is,
It is because it isn't
what it is not,
Inside the Rock the fossils
of our dreams,
Walking upon the water
We become Sevilla
And through subtle beings
of the air we contemplate,
Sitting between the fountain
and the Alcazar,
That's how we know it is,
there is no other is that is,
There is nothing to compare it to,
unto itself it is.

It has come to so many languages
Sounds and rhythms of the exact,
it is is, objecting the one,
That was song through a bird
captured by the power
of it,
Of it that it is.
It knows itself as such
and who has spoken its semblance,
An air that has become,
being word
Imagine just to be.
IT.

OLD MOVIES
—for Edward Dorn

Sometimes I see myself when I was someone else,
nights of crisp wind weaving through alien planets,
spot myself sitting on a roof posture toward
the Chrysler Building,
Bricks coming up or the frame is going down
through rusty texture. Feel myself as wind
through hallways pushing out to backyards.
Voyages flash scenarios before New York,
by a river of tropical curve,
the water streaming toward the motion of green.

I have surprised myself contained in pictures
as if I were the pair of eyes that beheld
Happenstance sitting across from myself on the
IRT the number 6 going uptown turning into
pollen fertilizing the wind the air that becomes
a language other than the visual letters of
this very ink like of knife
pages rippling tongues of recitation,
Watching bodies fall in front of sounds
a fever inhabited piercing right
to bone verbs, listen.
Action / Where a person I was once in a place
of whenland, a wardrobe and a vocabulary,
archived in deep recesses of the jaw molars
places and people a small opening in window
San Francisco chill makes interior become.
An aroma like a compass
a needle that points
toward a color or a room, a street, a walk,
a song passing radio car horse:
all the leaves are brown
and the sky is gray.
Again. In slow motion, frames held up
savored, sharp, crisp, I see the person I thought I knew.
Embarrassed humiliated the backdrop where the

wind has blown thorns here in the sudden wave
arrived on sand
The past furniture of my skin—
my bamboo flesh—near the river,
Riddle: What enters it and does not wet,
Shadow afternoon something walking
along the bank from bird's-eye view
Spectacular water snake apprehends the
frame,
A taste out of the horizon
the future ahead in the past gone,
prints me walking, leather coat
up 116th Street past First Avenue
toward the Greek pillars of
Benjamin Franklin High School
Alma Mater
Proximity to the East River
A fade out, the land around the river
Concretely vanishes street fish jump
for the new trees I swim the street
collide with island flora, women sitting
on rocks washing clothes, amphibious
creatures, cows, oxen, I am in Cambodian
countryside, the flower dance, equator bone,
the village people are silence,
the nymph girls talking is whispered prayer,
The clay mountain
before the urban winter,
the dream before territory,
The police of the nation nightmare.
Cut:
What texture I long for
running through the dark tunnels of sleep—
Imagine,
I am Bronze Age
Berber sitting at my craft,
Camels made of cellophane or papier
mâché color of papaya in a line down
a blond mound of Sahara sand,
I strive with feet and hands to move

closer screen, immobile, the sky a
blanket, appears a face,
returns me to religion, I bow
upon the prayer rug. Listen to the call
from the minaret, a row of men suddenly look
like ovals pressed against the earth.
I wake up in fragments.
Cut: action is what comes.
Streets and villages I rush through
buildings of burnt languages, ashes I
step upon,
A sound-administered genocide
in the marrow of bone.
Destiny turned age of seashells
into ruins,
Something the saliva of my
Tongue remembers the dormant
syllables.

The panel becomes a shaking camera
myself through a corridor someone's behavior
nauseating, shame rises runs through
my earth, I don't know if that
fool was me. Eye makes that frame fast speed
forward
A building printed in English
a mountain focused behind it
a twilight horizon a sun lizard
Spanish rising,
early crepuscular
Already the straw sombrero found
through microscope in gene blood jails
it was my grandfather suit white filament
drinking black coffee divine first light
ready to roll tobacco,
others more coarse machete to cut cane
harvest the world's sweetness.

Broken in Picasso's cubist slice
two faces

Each forming my features.
nothing is coordinated,
nose ear mouth floated together
antagonisms,
flesh color born of turmoil,
a scattered mind of lost
grandfathers
Listen up close.
I hear each insult my son imbibes
and like him the lights distract me,
I drown in a river of color and shape,
we bow our heads together
next to the shadows
Where we have been painted.

A cloud of gray moisture passes,
I inquire upon wicker Spanish sillón
facing vegetation mispronounced,
another color another focus
A portion of self folded against
blue and pink screaming plaster of
Paris walls and statue Saints begging
candlelight,
The Atmosphere is turbulence
and the present sunken mindless
Custom commotion,
frightened I want to escape
to someplace golden hot.

There in tenement chambers habitat
I historic
Looking like Persian little boy
neighbors all look like they came
from sunken Atlantis.

Schoolroom elemental jet-black hair
playing musical chairs with
foreigners in book language
Dick and Jane see Spot run,
the vortex of Babel,

the very vocabulary gives birth
to butterflies.
Scene becomes someone asleep
bed against wall window out
to middle air tenement shaft,
Coffee aromático orbits
Through new shift of legs searching
comfort brings me to the foot of
the mountains, an eye peeps
over it down to the aboriginals
in ceremony river baptism
bodies heads dipping into the water
back out different features,
I am the motions of Gladys my sister
humiliated by voices talk to them back,
we moved together to another language
together created sounds which were
between vocals us two riding the back
of a pickup truck father severe campesino
had us sit upon plantains and yucca
imported from Ecuador middle of
Manhattan, a hick of immediate
basic behavior. Bright stage lights
overwhelm the dancers into invisible
depths of archaeological sites
with the fossils of the caves,
where the words for fruits
are still the currency of the river
hidden by limestone.
Amidst it all the fresh wind full of
the past broken with a sudden role
of proyector a meridiana sea coast
comes in view over the
negation Manhattan skyline,
rooftop moving sideways on the frame,
a kind of yellowish light, beauty of smog,
the sound of tar stepped on by shoes
In the morning of the East River
tugboat horns,
Bricks cherry brownish rust

cement clay one atop another
reaching up pressing down upon the
bones of the Algonquin,
With thrown ears onto pavement, listen,
hear, the shuffling of brushing moccasins
of time's precedent within simulcast
analogous freedom stroll,
not far river the beef jerky
berries of summer wind eavesdrop
someone walking next to you,
Who might it be.

The reel jumps up, roaring mouths,
lions disguised with human faces,
want to eat you, however, I crumbled
amongst such horrors riding the train
stopping at destinies stations alien to
my habitat, it is midnight all this
belongs to me within the angles
of an Alfred Hitchcock movie, it was
that direction the falcon flew
unconcerned with my
true gentle nature and the stare
of a mad eye.

The hustlers of my youth were not
like the movies
Paul Newman, Jackie Gleason the felt
of the green pool table smooth,
When the camera rolled it showed
snakes pouring out of eyes,
mouths vapors of bats,
tongues like rats dizzy with selfish
destruction, black and white the
screen like photography in motion,
innocence eaten and chewed used
like a mannequin force obligates
to rip a happy face.
The men stood around watching the
chance rolls of the dice

crotch massaging the cruelty of their
crab.

From the moon the lens is focused,
I am an urban dancer within
psychiatric rooms a student of form
the nylon black of dresses the bolero
of the sleeves the bulge of the buttocks,
the Spanish eye Luis Buñuel slashes
in *Un chien andalou*—the Spanish dog
roams the night music stepping on
beats ablaze,
The sight of my Taino retina mixed
with the Granada Moors.
Talk about Weapons of Mass Destruction,
only missiles in Iraq are the
eyes of its beautiful women,
a beauty not perceived by the
northern killer military though
they profess manhood. Illustration that
burns.

I danced
with the Sumerians in the Bronx of my
Snaps my hands had sight serious
upon Mesoamericana waves,
lapis lazuli looming upon sapphire
shadows on the screen the indigo
thrown by the moon upon sofa
of rolling film.
Another slide I am closer to someone
I know,
An empire called California,
my face among the scattered mass,
enclosed within a Mission Victorian,
charming landscape of Dolores Park,
its palms no coco street after street
rising toward the open freeway.
In the play area my hands hold daughter
Rosa flower, swings toward new pyramid

building, slides down toward my face similitude.
In the sand she constructs castles.
At night the haze and blur,
too mellow for thought the scattered
stew, jungle faces, the distance now
focuses the illusion of golden epoch,
Watching the drying canvases emerging
from a cup in a café listening
to the Canto jondo depths
of the Guadalquivir rivulet.

A big white boat comes out of the bay,
I come aboard another language,
A Gypsy flow nomadic across Gibraltar
Straight.
My organs contain this fine wine,
from Rioja to Sale al Maghrib,
lens pictures within Café Ibn La Luna,
the liquid eyeball scanning
the *International Herald Tribune,*
unbelievable reports of cruelty,
A close-up pops frame of
the Gare de tren de Rabatville
Where a woman waits for a man.
The scenes they scatter back
into my pen the notebook
closed upon the table cinema
septima arte,
Onto the screen the word Fin
which sounds like Where
in Arabic / movie
Morocco sublime, a bird lands
on horseshoe archway
which looks like a keyhole,
Mina in my hands we filter
through the door opening: Beginning.

Colophon

The Mountain in the Sea was designed at Coffee House Press, in the historic warehouse district of downtown Minneapolis. The text is set in Bembo.

Funder Acknowledgments

Coffee House Press is an independent nonprofit literary publisher. Our books are made possible through the generous support of grants and gifts from many foundations, corporate giving programs, individuals, and through state and federal support. Coffee House Press receives general operating support from the Minnesota State Arts Board, through an appropriation by the Minnesota State Legislature and from the National Endowment for the Arts, a federal agency. Coffee House receives major funding from the McKnight Foundation, and from Target. Coffee House also receives significant support from: an anonymous donor; the Elmer and Eleanor Andersen Foundation; the Buuck Family Foundation; the Bush Foundation; the Patrick and Aimee Butler Family Foundation; the Foundation for Contemporary Arts; Gary Fink; Stephen and Isabel Keating; Seymour Kornblum and Gerri Lauter; the Lenfesty Family Foundation; Rebecca Rand; the law firm of Schwegman, Lundberg, Woessner & Kluth, P.A.; Charles Steffey and Suzannah Martin; the James R. Thorpe Foundation; the Archie D. and Bertha H. Walker Foundation; Thompson West; the Woessner Freeman Family Foundation; the Wood-Hill Foundation; and many other generous individual donors.

This activity is made possible in part by a grant from the Minnesota State Arts Board, through an appropriation by the Minnesota State Legislature and a grant from the National Endowment for the Arts.   MINNESOTA STATE ARTS BOARD   NATIONAL ENDOWMENT FOR THE ARTS   TARGET.

To you and our many readers across the country,
we send our thanks for your continuing support.

Good books are brewing at coffeehousepress.org